guitar
workout

Design: David Houghton

Music Engraving: Cambridge Notation
Music Transcription: David Mead
CD Production: Phil Hilborne at Widdle Studios, Essex

Printed by: MPG Books

Published by: Sanctuary Publishing Limited, 82 Bishops Bridge
Road, London W2 6BB

ISBN: 1 86074 239 4

guitar workout

David Mead

acknowledgments

Heartfelt thanks to:

Christine and the kids for putting up with 'Mr Grouch at the top of the stairs' whilst I was writing this book; to Phil Hilborne – the alphabet is not an adequate enough medium, etc etc – for a great-sounding CD, excellent cuisine and much encouragement in the studio; Dr James Cameron, for his advice while I was writing the chapter on music-related disorders, the *Guitar Techniques* team, Chris Francis, Jeff Hudson and Penny Braybrooke at Sanctuary Publishing, and all the pupils who have helped me learn so much about teaching guitar!

foreword

I got the idea for this book from the Canadian Airforce! Not all of them, of course – just the ones who published a ten-minute-a-day physical fitness schedule for modern times. The book took as its premise the fact that a lot of people needed some sort of fitness regime, but had little time to spare and certainly no time to attend a gym. It contained a series of graduated, graded exercises that would gradually bring about a good level of fitness (and therefore a reasonable expectation of good health) that relied on a time investment of only ten minutes per day.

From my own guitar teaching experience, I know that time is the biggest obstacle to students making progress on the instrument. After all, as John Lennon once astutely observed, 'Life is what happens while you're busy making other plans.' Mortgages, kids, work, commuting and sundry domestic duty all come before guitar practice... so what can you do?

I began to try to formulate a 'condensed' practice schedule for my busier students whereby they could cover many vital areas of learning in the shortest possible time and still see a satisfying result from their labour. I used a lot of feedback from pupils in developing this idea and in the end, we got quite good at it! The results have been decanted into this book – may it serve you well!

David Mead
January 1999

contents

Part One: Frequently Asked Questions

Part Two: The Guitar Gym

Part Three: Further Study

cd track listing

introduction

This book is essentially split into three parts. Part one sets out to clear up a lot of the uncertainties concerned with learning the guitar – frequently asked questions that I've collected from 17 years involved in teaching the instrument. Part two contains the workout mentioned in the title – and yes, it requires only ten minutes of your time on a daily basis. Part three is a lure into the innermost workings of music itself – an invitation to dip a toe, if you have a mind to – and, as such, contains more 'advanced' information.

In general, with the possible exception of some of the territory we wander into in part three, I'm trying to concentrate only on the things you need to know, not the things I want you to know just because *I* know them. A popular conceit amongst guitar teachers is that they feel that their pupils must know everything they do and do everything the way they do, too. I don't. I'll say here and now that I don't want you to play like me, I want you to play like *you*.

I learned most about what pupils expected from me when I found that the guys and gals sitting in front of me kept repeating the same thing; they just wanted to be able to go to a music store, buy a book of songs they wanted to play, go home and play them. Simple as that. It made me start to edit myself and say things like, 'But you don't need to know that....' It made my job a lot easier; I no longer felt I had to take people on musical safaris that they were unwilling to make. It occurred to me that plumbing the mysteries of what you could use a digital delay for was more interesting and pertinent than some of music's more arcane practices!

So we are going to spend a lot of time looking at the absolute bare essentials and, in the course of the next few weeks/months, I'm going to prove to you how you can get by quite happily thank-you without ever knowing what the Phrygian dominant mode is!

how to use this book

Learning guitar can be split into two different areas: physical and mental. The instrument places physical demands on the student from the outset (muscular/reflex development and co-ordination skills) and these can be addressed using a series of graduated 'chop-building' exercises which, if repeated regularly, will build a student's facility to deal with this area.

Music skills have to be learned, too; the analogy here is that the physical side of playing is like learning to type, whereas learning music will give you something to say at the end of it!

In some ways, it's probably a good idea for you to proceed straight to part two of the book and get on with the exercises, using part one to fill in any blanks about chords, scales, effects units, reading tablature or whatever as you wish. Guitar playing is fairly addictive and so I've no doubt your curiosity will be aroused in certain areas – I trust I've thought of most of the answers!

I've taken the opportunity to provide you with CD examples of as much as possible in order to better get various points across – plus a few backing tracks to practise with, if you so wish.

The best advice I can offer is to stick with the exercise plan while you explore the instrument and shape your own 'guitar destiny' as you go. As ever, the most important thing is to have fun!

questions, questions...

I've already said, of course, that we're going to keep things very lean in this book – essential stuff only, remember – and much of the first part you'll read is concerned with some commonly asked questions about learning the guitar. They're the major questions, as far as I'm concerned, but I thought that it would be a good idea to sort out some of the more minor niggles, too. So this chapter is going to take the form of an FAQ – or frequently asked questions – much beloved of computer jargonists everywhere!

How do I keep this damn thing in tune?

Tuning is an all-important fundamental as far as learning guitar is concerned and one where we cannot turn to the professional for advice – or can we? Most pro players rely on a pair of finely-tuned ears to sort their tuning dilemmas out; you've seen the sort of thing, a guitarist will be seen to tweak a couple of the tuning pegs of his guitar very casually – usually while he introduces the next number! He's not being a smartass, he just knows what he's doing, that's all. Obviously it can take a fair old time to attune your ears to the peak of perfection and we're interested in instant results, right? So, go and buy a tuner. Simple as that. I apologise for telling you you've got to open your purse or wallet already (although I'm hopefully going to save you some cash in the chapter about gear, so don't be too hard on me just yet).

Electronic tuners come in a variety of shapes and sizes but they all do the same essential job – they keep your guitar happily in tune with itself (and the rest of the world) which is not only good for you (because you should NEVER practise on an out-of-tune guitar) but it's good for those of a sensitive nature who might just have to occupy the same space as you do.

Just plug the guitar in, tune each string until the gadget tells you you're on target, and then get down to business. Couldn't be simpler, really, could it? A lot of pros use electronic tuners, too; sometimes relying on your ears, however good, on a noisy stage is far from a failsafe path towards perfect harmony (or melody, for that matter).

Electronic tuners are things that I have personally had a big change of heart about in recent years – as a teacher and player. I used to recommend pupils buy nothing more fancy than a tuning fork and learn (painstakingly in some cases) to tune the guitar from that. But having used a tuner myself for a number of years, I've softened somewhat – seduced by their simplicity and accuracy. I do know of one guitarist, incidentally, who tunes his guitar with an electronic tuner and then uses his ears to get it perfect... but he's got a musical ear which is probably not of this earth!

How long before I can play to a reasonable level?

Well, if you've trusted me enough to buy this book because I've promised the shortest possible route between point A (ie you, now) and point B (ie you when you can play quite nicely) then I'm not going to lie to you now! The guitar is not an instrument from which it is fair to expect any kind of instant results. It's a hard taskmaster and ranks with the most difficult instruments to play well. On the other hand, I've proved to absolute beginners that they can play something after their first lesson, even if it is only a simple chord change or two. It depends on your expectations; by all means set your sights as high as you want; Rodrigo Guitar Concerto? Eric Clapton's famous 'Crossroads' solo? Not a problem, it's just going to take time, that's all. If you can learn to be a little patient and be satisfied with the tried-and-tested route of setting yourself short-term, achievable goals, then you'll find that the little you progress each day/week/month is, one day, going to add up to a lot!

A lot of things depend on how quickly you can overcome some of the physical barriers that the guitar throws up. As an example, I can tell you how to play a barre chord, and recommend that you learn to play them as soon as you can, but you need to develop certain muscles, etc before they become physically possible. The important thing is not to regard this sort of thing as an insuperable obstacle and give up. Practise your weak areas and get on with something else in the meantime.

If you're still expecting a one-sentence answer to the above question, incidentally, then let me say that I played my first gig when I had been playing 13 months – and I'm nothing terribly special!

Can anyone play or do you have to be 'born with it'?

Ah, the old, 'Some are born great, others achieve greatness and some have greatness thrust upon them' chestnut! Listen; here's my philosophy on this one. If there are any geniuses in the guitar world, I've probably met them via my day job as guitar magazine editor. We do that kind of thing, it's nice. If there has been anything in common with these gentlemen (and remember that 'genius' is a highly subjective word to throw in any direction) it is a dedication that goes way beyond what many of us would consider 'normal'. Unless you call practising for six or seven hours a day, every day, come rain or shine and no matter what's on telly, 'normal'! I think that these gentlemen (and ladies) are born with an insatiable musical curiosity which luck, circumstances and many other factors all play a part in shaping – I can assure you that raw talent is not an access-all-areas pass to success.

However – have we established yet that not everyone who plays guitar wants to play at pro level? (Or even play in public.) And so my answer to the above (pretty common) question is, Yes, of course anyone can play – and play well. Anyone who wants to conquer the instrument passionately enough isn't going to let a few minor obstacles like playing barre chords stop them, after all.

Do I need big hands or long fingers to be able to play well?

No. I've taught people with all manner of hand/finger shapes and sizes and everyone has found their way into playing. I had one pupil who had broken her fingers when she was young and was afraid that the fact that they hadn't set dead straight would hold back her progress on the instrument. It didn't. If ever I am confronted by someone who wants to blame some minor (and usually imagined) physical 'handicap' for their lack of progress, I usually do two things: one, I make a mental note that their interest could be waning and make a special effort to be more encouraging (which doesn't come naturally to a cynical, grouchy old bastard like me). And two, I tell them the story of the late jazz guitarist Django Reinhardt whose hand was very badly burned in a house fire which caused some of the muscles in his right hand to wither – it was a terrible injury, believe me, especially for a guitarist. He had two fingers which he could use to play with and he could sometimes get away with playing with a combination of his third and little fingers for chords. Anyway, the doctors suggested he should continue to play as a form of physiotherapy and he became an absolute legend on the instrument! In fact there are plenty of us who are fully complemented in the finger department who cannot approach some of the things Django did with only two and a bit. So no wimping out just because you think your fingers are too short, long or fat!

Can someone really teach themselves to play?

Ultimately, *everyone* teaches themselves to play! Even if you decide to go to a teacher for lessons, it's your decision and if you make the fullest possible use of that teacher you will get from him only the information you need to achieve your ambitions with the instrument. You're in charge, remember! A good teacher will put him/herself completely at the service of his pupil and steer them in the direction that suits them.

I used to make a bargain with my pupils; I'd say that as long as they practised what I asked them to (mainly technical exercises to develop their hands, etc) and spent a few minutes playing over the stuff with me during their lesson, then the rest of the time was theirs. If they wanted me to transcribe a tape, then so be it. If they wanted to look at a particular technique, we got on with it there and then. The pupils who didn't keep their side of the bargain and didn't practise what I'd recommended found that they were wasting a lot of their own time by having me go over exercises with them time and time again, week after week, perhaps leaving only ten minutes at the end of an hour to look at a song. Most of them complied! I thought it was a fair enough bargain, after all. Cruel, perhaps, but fair!

I'm left-handed, so I need a left-handed guitar, right?

Not necessarily! Once again, if I could get to a left-handed pupil soon enough, I'd recommend most strongly that they tried to play the 'conventional' way round. There are so many arguments and so much controversy about this single fact; there is a school of thought which says that there is no such thing as a left-handed piano, so why should there be a left-handed guitar? Violinists, cellists, double-bass players are taught to play the same way irrespective of their left or right handedness, why should guitarists be different? There are very, very few classical guitarists who play 'the other way round' and so it's just a question of orienteering, right?

My own perspective on the great left-handed guitar debate is that a beginner faces a lot of physical problems to overcome in the early days of learning guitar – holding the thing correctly is a step in itself. So orienteering him or herself to play the conventional way round might as well be one of those problems!

To come over all scientific for a moment, I've been told that left or right-handedness is never 100% in anyone anyway; we are merely biased one way or the other to varying degrees. If you're 50% either way, they tell you that you're ambidextrous. If you're 75% biased towards right-handedness then you still may perform a few tasks with your left hand and feel quite natural doing so. It's true the other way round, too. I'm a case in point; I write with my right hand, but do loads of other things quite naturally with my left – throw darts, play ping-pong, bowl a cricket ball, etc. So my own degree of right or left handedness is probably near equal but only slightly biased towards my right hand.

A left-handed player has a big advantage to playing the conventional way round, too. The left hand is expected to do some quite tricky manoeuvring on the fretboard, wouldn't it be better if your right or left bias was best spent there? Certainly Mark Knopfler, Joe Pass and Gary Moore must have thought so because they are all left-handed!

At the end of the day, my advice to a left-handed person just starting out on the guitar would be to try and play the 'right' way round. If, after a few months, it really feels wrong, then OK, buy a left-handed guitar – but it's really better to persevere!

And, before you ask, Hendrix was actually right-handed...

Chapter 2

have I got the right gear?

You've probably already got a guitar and are frustrated by the fact that it doesn't make all those great noises that you hear on CDs. A lot of people will actually blame the guitar for this, but let's get one thing absolutely clear from the outset; there are no great guitarists, just great musicians who happen to play guitar! An awful lot of a guitarist's 'sound', his choice of notes, phrasing and so on comes from his musical soul and not an assorted jumble of wood and wire.

The guitar is like a typewriter – it's a communication tool, nothing more. In the same way that a typewriter can be responsible for great novels or complete drivel, so can the guitar! The most crucial variable in the equation is you. I've seen so many people blame their guitar for sounding bad and make the big mistake of rushing out and buying a really expensive guitar and amp to match only to find that they still sound bad. Once again, the guitar is a tool – and we're trying to turn you into a good enough musician to use that tool properly.

That's not to say, of course, that it's not good to love your instrument; I've had plenty of conversations with people who are in love with their guitars and are ridiculed by their entire family for sitting there looking at it longingly! We're not mad because of this, the guitar is just that kind of instrument, that's all.

I thought it might be helpful to run through a little bit on the whys and wherefores of equipment, offering some pointers and advice along the way. I'm not going to put you off the idea of one day owning the very Rolls Royce of guitars, but, in the interest of our lean, mean approach to everything in this book, it might be interesting to see what are the minimum requirements you should expect from any piece of gear.

Guitars

Guitars come in all shapes, sizes and types. I would think that guitarists, people who write for guitar magazines and teachers are asked the question, 'Which sort of guitar should I buy?' more often than any other. The first bit of sound, solid advice is to look seriously at what sort of music/guitar playing you like listening to. I've been asked on plenty of occasions if it was OK to start learning on electric guitar, or would it be better to start on acoustic guitar and work 'upwards'. This is based on the erroneous idea that acoustic guitars are cheaper than electrics. Now this might have been true once upon a time, but not any more. I don't think anyone would give me much of an argument if I said that it actually costs more to make a good acoustic guitar than it does a good electric. So my response to the question would be that if you like listening principally to electric guitarists, then by all means buy an electric guitar.

An acoustic guitar is, in the end, not more difficult to play than an electric – in fact the techniques involved are, in some instances, quite different between the two. So it should be a fairly easy equation to answer; if you enjoy listening to electric guitars, buy an electric right away, if it's acoustic music that captures your imagination, buy an acoustic. If it's classical guitar, then bear with me a while and we'll get round to talking about that, too!

Electric guitars

There are quite a few variations on the theme which we should take a brief look at, but first things first. It's probably sensible to set yourself a budget before you look at anything and try to stick to it. The current manufacturing strategy in the guitar industry is to try and provide an instrument to fit any purse, and the advice here is quite simple; ask around as to which are the 'better makes' of instrument, invest in a couple of guitar magazines and read the reviews to see which points to look for and, if you can, take someone along to the shop with you who already plays. A good guitar teacher will be prepared to come along with you (he might charge you the same as a lesson for his services) because it's in his interests as much as yours that you get a good instrument. You're going to be easier to teach on a guitar you don't have to fight against all the time! I did this a few times with people (and still do, occasionally).

So your first electric is quite likely to be a 'budget' model. Don't feel that you're a second-hand citizen in the guitar world because you've bought from the budget range – there are plenty of guitars out there which are quite modestly priced and that are really good instruments. (If you need any further reassurance, I recorded some of the accompanying CD using a guitar which cost me only £130 and I've NEVER paid more than £600 for a guitar in my life!)

In order to narrow your choice of instrument down still further, there are a few finer points that we're going to look at. It's a case of asking yourself that initial question once again; what sort of music do you like to listen to or want to play? Certain styles of music demand certain different characteristics which it might be well to be aware of from the start.

Heavy rock

Of course, there's not really any such thing as the standard heavy rock guitar – there are exceptions to every rule, remember. But in general, rock guitars tend to be solid-bodied, with perhaps a

locking tremolo system and humbucking pickups. Ignore all the niceties like colour, finish and whether it's got go-faster stripes and cool-looking pointy bits, we're worried about basics here, nothing more.

Be aware that guitars are a bit like cars in that the more features you have on them (like a locking trem, for instance) the more the price goes up. As in everything, you get what you pay for and to begin with you are more worried about the actual playability of the instrument rather than what toys it has installed. As long as the actual 'playing area' (fretboard, nut, bridge, etc) is up to scratch, you'll get on fine. If you go for an instrument which appears to have all the frills for very little money, you'll end up regretting it.

Rock and blues

It's probably worth talking briefly about guitar history at this point. Just briefly. Most of the electric guitars that you find hanging on music shop walls today owe their existence to instruments designed during the 1950s. In the guitar halls of fame there are but two major players: the Fender Stratocaster and the Gibson Les Paul. When I edited *Guitarist* magazine, we used to contend that you only really needed two electric guitars in order to produce every recorded guitar sound – a Strat and a Les Paul. (The Fender Telecaster also received an honourable mention, incidentally.) Of course, we were being almost impossibly general (and probably a little elitist, too), but there was an essential truth running through the idea, all the same. But everything else was a matter of fine tuning; you can get guitars which are vaguely Strat-shaped but have twin humbucking pickups – essentially a hybrid between the two fundamental designs.

Having said all that (and I think I deserve some credit for the fact that I summed up the entire history of electric guitar design in one paragraph!) the choice of which instrument you choose to play rock or blues on is literally in your hands. Take a look at what your favourite players have in theirs! Remember, most designs of guitar have a budget version available – for instance, Epiphone make a very respectable Les Paul (under licence from Gibson) and Fender have their own budget Stratocaster under the Squier banner.

For rock and blues, we're talking solid bodies again – although more and more bands are taking up semi-acoustics, based on Gibson's 335 design. I'm not going to comment here other than to recommend that you beware the fickle fancies of fashion...

Jazz

I don't think I'm going to upset anyone unduly if I say that jazz players are a traditional lot and, hence, tend towards traditional instruments.

Jazz guitarists started (way back in the 30s and 40s) playing acoustic guitars. The guitar was never considered to be a soloing instrument and it was hence confined to playing a subordinate, rhythmic role in big bands. During the 40s, experiments with electric guitars started and, thanks mainly to a guitarist called Charlie Christian, the guitar sprang out of the backline and up to the front. At last you could hear what the guitarist was playing! When the electromagnetic guitar pickup was fully designed and realised, jazz players started leaping out of the woodwork from every direction. But they still wanted their instruments to retain a great many of the characteristics of their old acoustics; hollow bodies, arched tops, f-holes, wooden bridges and heavy gauge strings. To a certain extent, jazz guitar design was halted right there! There have been some refinements along the way, of course, but if you sneak a look through the jazz racks in the local record shops, you'll find that, in the main, most of the current instruments are very similar to their forbears.

So, if jazz is your thing, you buy an archtop electro-acoustic, right? Well, probably not, actually. Let me explain. This type of guitar is phenomenally expensive to build properly and, unless you want a price tag in excess of £1000, I would recommend that you start your jazz guitar explorations with a straightforward acoustic guitar. If, at sometime in the future, you decide it's worth the investment, you'll find that having played acoustic guitar will stand you in excellent stead for the switchover to archtop. It will feel familiar and respond similarly – most importantly, you'll have saved yourself a lot of money and frustration fighting with inferior instruments until you're sure that jazz is the direction for you. We'll be talking about acoustics in a few paragraphs!

Country

Country guitar players are a fairly traditional lot, too. The Fender Telecaster has pretty much become synonymous with country and, it's true to say that, an awful lot of the sounds you hear on country albums past and present originated on just that instrument. Of course, that's a whacking great generalisation and certain country archivists will probably come looking for me wanting to string me up, but in this case, I feel the generalisation is more than justified!

There are exceptions to the rule, of course; Chet Atkins doesn't play a Tele and he is one of the most well-known country players on the planet. But many do. It's something to do with the unique pickup layout on a Tele that gives it its country voice; two single-coils, the bridge pickup is bright and punchy, the neck pickup smooth and mellow (so much so in fact that many jazz players have bought Teles).

So the aspiring country player doesn't have to look around too much to place himself right in the country ball park! But don't take my word for it – have a look around at your favourite players and see. If you can't identify which guitar is which, find a picture and take it to a guitar shop and they'll put you straight.

Pop

Now we've really got problems in the pop department. Don't forget that the pop world is irrevocably linked to trends and fashions and so I'm not even going to try any generalisation here. Anything I recommend could just be out of date by the time I've finished this sentence! In a way, this is quite frustrating, but it can actually work in your favour. Anything goes, right? So you can't really go wrong if you remember my basic advice: don't look at guitars that cost a fortune, try to take someone who plays with you (preferably not someone who has only been playing a couple of months, please) just to make sure that whatever you buy is actually playable and not a complete dog. You should be OK; pop, remember, has an ever-changing face and very few staples.

Points to watch out for...

If someone was to ask the question, 'What should I look out for when I'm buying my first electric guitar?' I'd have to admit that it's an almost impossible question to answer. Part of the problem lies with the fact that you need to know what you're looking for in order to find it! It's just like buying a car; initially, you are in the hands of the salesperson and you have to trust them and the after-sales service they're offering. In a perfect world, of course, all would be well – and I have no doubt to think otherwise. But it might be worth offering just a few words of caution, all the same.

Modern manufacturing processes (and this isn't just confined to the guitar market, it could apply equally well to fridges, hi-fi or any other domestic consumable) are generally good and quality of production these days is hundreds of times better than it was ten years ago. But you do get the occasional problem, it has to be said. Realistically, the things to watch out for are concerned with the instrument's playability and cosmetic standard. Anyone can check out the cosmetics at a glance, you don't really need to be an expert to find dents, chips or finish checks (as they're known). Give the instrument a good going over first to make sure that there aren't any marks that you would find it impossible to live with when you get the guitar home. Guitars do show signs of wear after only a little while anyway.

Neck

Then you need to be fairly sure that the neck is straight – if it isn't, you'll suffer tuning and intonation problems and probably some buzzes and rattles when the strings are held down to fret a note, too. It's absolutely impossible to tell someone how to 'sight' a neck to see if it's straight with no experience – this is certainly an area where taking someone along with you who has some prior experience or even a smattering of expert knowledge would be of definite help to you. Having said that, minor aberrations as far as neck straightness can be easily adjusted by an experienced hand and so don't panic if someone tells you that a bit of tweaking might be necessary, neck-wise. I've always thought of buying a guitar as being similar to buying a suit; you generally need a

few nips and tucks before the thing actually fits!

Check how the neck feels in your hands, too. There are thin necks, thick, chunky necks and a few different fingerboard radiuses to come to terms with, too. The radiusing of a fingerboard means how curved it is from bass side to treble. Older guitars (like 50s Stratocasters, for instance) had quite a curve to them – a 71/4 inch radius, if you're interested. If you're really interested, borrow a set of compasses from somewhere (I say 'borrow' it's not the sort of thing I would expect you to have to hand!), measure out a radius of seven and a quarter inches and draw an arc. That's how curved that particular fingerboard is going to be. Repeat the experiment for 91/2 and you'll be surprised how much flatter the fingerboard will look. Some modern guitars have fingerboards which are almost flat. It's probably an almost meaningless point to raise at this early stage, but it can make a big difference to the feel of a guitar – and just mentioning neck radius or 'camber' in a guitar shop might just give you a couple of extra brownie points with the sales staff!

Action

Next, check to see how high the strings appear above the fretboard. Guitarists call this the 'playing action' or 'action' for short. Obviously, it takes more effort to push down a string which is quite far above the fretboard – and high action can sometimes be a warning sign to other problems, so beware.

OK, so how high is high? Or, more importantly, what's normal? Basically, a medium (ie perfectly all right) action would have the bass string (the one nearest you in the normal playing position) sitting about 4/64 of an inch above the 12th fret – that's from the top of the fret to the underside of the string. The treble E would probably be expected to check in at about 2/64ths or 3/64ths of an inch. Understand that these measurements are only intended as a guide and are by no means set in stone. I don't intend, either, that you should carry a steel rule about with you on your guitar purchasing mission. I'm merely giving you some idea of what a regular action would look like. If it's really *much* higher than this, then it's still adjustable and any good shop will offer to alter it or 'set the guitar up' for you. But every so often, you find a guitar which, when you try lowering the action, won't play properly because of the cumulative effects of other problems, some of which could be costly to put right. If in doubt, walk away – or at least insist on some kind of expert second opinion.

Electrics

This bit is relatively easy. No measurements to worry about here, just simply plug the guitar into an amp in the shop and make sure that you can get a sound out of it! Adjust the pickup selector (or 'toggle switch', to invoke the vernacular!) and make sure you still get something in all positions. Play with the volume and tone controls to make sure they don't crackle and, if everything seems to work, all is probably well.

It really is a good idea to have somebody with you who plays at this point, too. I know I keep rattling on about this, but it could just save you a little bit of heartache. If you simply don't know anyone who plays, then ask one of the guys/gals in the shop to play it for you while you listen. Believe me, guys/gals who work in music shops are only too delighted to demonstrate guitars and many have got a few party pieces stashed away that they're simply dying to show you! (And, before you ask, I did work in a music shop once.)

If everything looks, feels and sounds OK, then you're probably safe in parting with your cash. It might be prudent to enquire about what sort of back-up the shop is prepared to offer you in case something happens later on, though.

If I seem to be painting a particularly glum picture of guitar retail outlets, I'm not; I'm really only describing a worst possible case scenario and it's nothing more than suggesting you look both ways before crossing the road and brushing your teeth after every meal!

Acoustic guitars

As I said earlier, acoustic guitars are, in general, harder to make well than their electric counterparts. Only because modern mass-production techniques don't really suit this type of instrument – too much craft has to go into the building process. This is not to say that it's impossible to buy a budget acoustic; of course you can. But build and the overall quality of materials

are crucial to the end result – the production of good tone.

Everything I've said already about action, finish, necks and so on applies to an acoustic instrument, too – probably doubly inasmuch that adjustment is not always quite so user-friendly. It's unusual to find an adjustable bridge on an acoustic, for instance and so, if the action is high (although it is generally expected to be higher than an electric guitar) it's going to mean a trip to the workshop to have it altered.

Acoustics have a variety of different body shapes, based mainly on the traditional 'figure 8' shape. If I was to run out another of my generalisations here, I would say that body sizes come in large (sometimes called 'jumbos' or 'Dreadnoughts'), medium or small. The small-bodied acoustics are sometimes referred to as being 'parlour guitars' which is a particularly quaint term from around the turn of the century (18/1900s) and the traditionalist inside me is really glad it survived!

Your choice of body size is down to you. It's logical to assume, of course, that the larger the body, the 'louder' or 'fuller' the guitar is going to sound – simple physics tells us the reasons for that. But, frustratingly, it's not always true! I've played plenty of small-bodied guitars which are both remarkably loud and full-sounding and a good many big-bodied guitars which you can hardly hear six feet away!

You'll discover a lot about the variety of tones on offer from an acoustic by playing a few of them – or having them played to you. Strangely enough, it's not always best to judge the sound of an acoustic guitar when you're the one who is sitting and playing it. Many instruments of this sort really only come into their own a few feet away (a bit like a twelve-bore shotgun!). Try as many as you can before you think about buying, the research will be worth it.

A couple of other tips when buying acoustics would be to look inside the soundhole and make sure that everything looks neat and tidy inside. If this area is quite 'clean' you can be pretty sure the manufacturer observed a good standard of workmanship in other areas, too. If the inside has got uneven-looking joints and great blobs of glue all over the place, maybe we can assume the opposite, huh?

Make sure the top of the guitar is flat with no irregular bumps, dips, warps or bulges, particularly behind the bridge.

Of course, the humble acoustic would have to be miked up (ie you would have to play through a microphone/PA set-up) if you were thinking about performing in public with a band and so it may be worth checking out the next paragraph before you fully make your mind up!

Electro-acoustics

An electro-acoustic will have a built-in pickup which enables you to plug it into either a special acoustic amp or straight into a PA in order to perform live. Now, I probably don't have to tell you that this makes the instrument's price-band even more sensitive, do I? We're introducing a system of electronic gadgetry which is pretty expensive in its own right, before it's added to the cost of manufacture of the guitar which will be its host.

One thing you need to sort out before choosing between an acoustic or electro-acoustic is in which form the guitar will get the most use. If you're going to be using the guitar mainly at home with the distant prospect of doing a couple of gigs.... maybe, then I'd stick to a bog standard acoustic. Remember, you'll be paying more for all the electronic gubbins.

But if you've got your heart set on playing live, it's maybe a good idea to take a look at a few electro-acoustics. Run through all the checks I've outlined above, but make sure that you get to listen to the guitar in both its sound environments. You may find that you like it amplified, but it's a bit weak acoustically or the other way round. To be honest, an electro-acoustic is always going to be a compromise; there is a big difference between building a guitar with a soundbox as the heart of its voice and a guitar which will live most of its life being heard via a pickup – and the best of both worlds is a tough trick to pull off.

Classical guitars

The classical guitar is the ancestor of the modern day electric or acoustic. This type of guitar started turning up around 400 years ago in one form or the other, dropping in and out of favour and fashion, finally enjoying a renaissance in the early to mid 1900s. It's strange to think that it's only recently that the classical instrument has been taken in any way seriously by the world to which it belongs. At one time, the idea of playing Bach on a guitar was considered blasphemous by the classical music establishment, and it's only really the efforts, perseverance and combined genius of players like André Segovia, Julian Bream and John Williams who have established the instrument as one worthy of being taken seriously.

Non-orchestral instruments are traditionally given a hard time – you've only got to look at the reputation of the saxophone to see another instrument which has fallen into the big divide between 'serious' and 'spurious'. There are still some classical musicians who treat the sax like it was some sort of ornate kazoo!

So, for a long time, the guitar enjoyed 'folk' or even 'gypsy' status amongst other instruments, but, as I said, it was rescued from the outpourings of bile being aimed at it from the classical fraternity by some very special talents indeed.

These days, the repertoire for the classical guitar is still not huge – composers need to know the workings of the guitar before being able to plumb its depths compositionally – and much of the music played upon the instrument is culled from elsewhere. It's not uncommon to hear music originally written for the cello, lute or harpsichord played in a guitar recital, for instance.

The classical guitar is a demanding instrument to learn and one has to decide straight away to conform to its strict disciplines or all is lost. But a great deal of guitarists just fall in love with the sound of the classical guitar; its nylon strung, quiet voice often turns up in the rock'n'roll arena, too.

If you're starting out and want to end up playing rock or pop, it's probably not a good idea to begin playing a classical guitar – despite the fact that classical guitars to seem to be available at a price well below acoustic or electrics. There are major differences between the classical and 'popular' models and I for one am a staunch believer that you should, as far as possible, start as you mean to continue. So if you are considering a course which will take you into the areas of pop, folk, country, rock, blues or jazz, then I would advise you to steer a conventional course from the beginning. Whether or not to own a classical guitar is a decision you can safely leave until later on.

I've already said that making an acoustic guitar well is more difficult than making an electric. Well, a classical instrument is probably even more difficult again and one would do well to avoid what may seem at first to be a 'good deal' on a new instrument of this sort.

Incidentally, it used to be thought that you could pick up a classical guitar 'cheap' and make it sound more like a regular acoustic guitar by putting steel strings on it. One word: don't! The difference in tension between nylon and steel strings is enormous and you will almost certainly ruin the guitar. I speak from experience; I once ignored all the advice I was given and put a set of steel strings on a classical guitar and the neck came off! I'd like to think that I could prevent someone else making that mistake if I can.

Electro-classical

Just as there are acoustic guitars with built-in pickups hidden away inside, so too are there classical guitars aimed at live performance. Let's get one thing straight – you're not likely to see a classical guitarist playing one of these little beasties during a recital. Top of the range classical guitars are made in such away that they are acoustically loud enough for the concert hall – electro-classicals are aimed more at the popular end of the market. Once again, you can expect to pay quite a bit more for the convenience of an on-board pickup system on your nylon string and so it's only worth considering if you really believe this is the way it's going to lead most of its useful, playing life.

Strings

You would think that there might not be too much of a story to tell about strings. They're not exactly glamorous, after all. But I've witnessed a fair amount of confusion concerning them and so it's worth saying a few words on their behalf.

Strings are doubtlessly the guitarist's greatest consumable. Nearly all the pro players I've ever spoken to change their strings before every gig and if you're a hard-working player, that can add up to a fair amount of cash per year. So what sort of strings are right for you?

Electric guitar strings

When you buy your guitar, it's more than likely to be fitted with a set of strings which we colloquially refer to as 'nines'. That is, the top E string measures in at .009 of an inch in diameter and it has fallen into the guitar playing vocabulary that the top string gives a whole set its name.

A 'set of nines' will, in fact, look like this:

Top E	=	.009
B	=	.011
G	=	.016
D	=	.024
A	=	.032
Bass E	=	.042

Another way of describing the above string set to other interested parties would be 'nine to 42s'.

For whatever reason, this has become known as the default set of strings in the electric guitar world. It's probably down to the simple fact that it is by far the most popular. But strings come in a number of different gauges. The only 'lighter' or thinner gauge available starts with a top E weighing in at .008 – how much difference can one thousandth of an inch make? Well, quite a lot, actually! You will definitely notice quite a lot of difference between the two sets.

Similarly, the next set up will feel quite different, too. We go up another thou to a top string measuring .010 and I guarantee you'll notice the difference immediately.

Theoretically speaking, it's possible to go up to .013 as a top E (and beyond if you've got bionic fingers) but as you increase string mass expect two things to happen: one, your strings will be more and more difficult to bend and two, your guitar might sound like it's actually got louder! The explanation for the second phenomenon is pure electromagnetics; the more mass the string possesses whilst vibrating in the pickup's magnetic field, produces more current being fed into your amp. A lot of guitarists will tell you that the overall tone is improved into the bargain.

So does this mean you have to experiment with strings when you start playing? No. Stick with 'nines' to start with; you can make decisions about going up in gauge when you've gained a little playing experience. That way, you'll be able to recognise the benefits and disadvantages and make a better decision. I'm really giving you all the above information to save a bit of confusion when it's time for a string change and you go into a music store and ask for a packet of strings. You'd be surprised how taken aback some early guitar players are when they're asked which gauge string they use!

How often do you change strings?

I'll deal with this one now, before we look at acoustic and nylon strings, because I have it in the back of my mind that you would-be electric players aren't going to bother to read the next couple of sections and I don't want you to miss anything!

There is no set time to change strings; nothing is written in stone and, of course, it's down to how often you play and for how long. Believe it or not, body chemistry can influence string life wildly. I don't pretend to understand anything about biochemistry (do you think I'd play guitar if I did?), but my layman's knowledge tells me that some people produce sweat which is more 'corrosive' than others. I've seen it for myself; I've had pupils who practise daily and work quite hard at it, but can keep a set of strings in pristine condition for weeks. Others will get through a set in a matter of days or even hours!

How do you know when a set of strings is finished? It's a bit like chewing gum losing its flavour; there's a point when you give up and throw the gum away and that point varies from person to person. What happens to strings is similar, but strings lose their tone, as opposed to flavour. You can hear the difference between a brand new set and an old set at once; the new set is full of life with quite a clear, ringing top end. By comparison, the old set is dull and lifeless – the time to change strings is just before they finally lose all their bright quality, but, as I've already pointed out, that will vary from one person to another.

You can do a lot to preserve string life by wiping them over with a cloth after every practice or playing session – pretty much nobody I know ever does, but they all know they're meant to and so I thought I'd pass it on!

Do strings break often?

Again, this will vary enormously between players. I've heard it said that good players don't break strings, but I think that's a myth! I don't break that many and here's where reasonably regular string changes can help. Strings wear out. Fact. Constant bending and bashing against the frets will do sufficient damage to ensure that one day something's got to give. Metal fatigue plays its part, too.

If you find that you're breaking an awful lot of strings, it's probably a good idea to take a serious look at your playing technique (don't blame the guitar!). If you're being too heavy handed in the picking or strumming departments, you either need to learn to hold back a little or go up a string gauge.

One final piece of advice in our string section would be to have someone show you how to change your strings the first time you need to change them. And learn how to do it properly yourself as soon as you can. I always used to change pupils' strings for them during a regular lesson (only when it needed doing, of course!) because it used to save time making sure that they were put on properly and weren't going to cause unnecessary problems when I wasn't there to put things right. When pupils realised that it was going to eat up about 20 minutes of their lesson, they soon wanted to learn to do it properly themselves!

Acoustic guitar strings

There are two main differences between acoustic and electric strings: one is that acoustic strings tend to be of a heavier gauge in general and two is their appearance is slightly different, too.

The heavier gauge is because of a couple of things. We're no longer relying on electromagnetics to produce our sound and so, in a lot of ways, acoustic strings have to work harder. A greater string mass will vibrate more air which, in turn, will produce more volume and a more controlled tone. They look different because acoustic guitar strings invariably include a wound third (ie G). This is because of G's pitch to mass ratio and you'll forgive me if I hold my hands up here and say that I'm in no way scientific enough to give you a proper explanation. I'll generalise (because I'm good at that) and say that winding the G gives it more stability and helps to produce a good, steady pitch. How come we can get away with an unwound G on an electric? It's down to compromise, really; as far as this mass/pitch equation goes, an unwound G is a borderline case, but because rock guitar players couldn't possibly live without bending the G at every conceivable opportunity, it's easier on their fingertips to leave it unwound. This isn't the case for acoustic players; the acoustic instrument's playing vocabulary doesn't include quite so much bending and so we can afford to be generous, give the G its due and wind it!

I said that acoustic string gauges tend to be a bit heavier and it's true. It shows up when you consider that the default gauge on an electric might be seen as 'a set of nines', but on an acoustic guitar even .010s are considered fairly flunky!

Once again, you'll eventually settle on a gauge which feels right for you and a little experimentation when the time comes won't go amiss.

Nylon strings

In some ways, nylon, or classical guitar strings are the easiest to sum up. Gauge isn't an issue here, thanks mainly to the standardisation of classical guitar design, and so for once, you're reasonably safe asking for a set of nylon strings without the bother of having to qualify your request or supply any further information.

Later on, you will find that nylon strings come in different 'tensions' but I'm safe in saying that you'll have to be reasonably far down the classical guitar line before it really becomes something you'll need to worry about.

In general – and this applies to all strings – don't buy cheap as tuning stability is of prime importance and cheap strings do tend to go out of tune more often than their more expensive counterparts. Remember that strings have an awful lot to do with your tone and you certainly don't want to skimp in that department.

Amplifiers

One thing's for sure; if you're going to play electric guitar, you're going to need an amplifier. Many people think that it is necessary that the two, amp

and guitar, come as a package or are at least bought at the same time. Well, I didn't do things that way; there was a year between purchases and I don't think it did me an enormous amount of harm. That might come as a surprise to a lot of people who may be thinking, 'What's the point of having an electric guitar without being able to hear it?' But it's true. I still do the vast amount of my day to day practice or noodling without my guitar plugged into an amp. Of course you *can* hear an electric guitar when it's not plugged in, it's just that not many other people can! When you think about it, doesn't that suit many domestic situations nicely? You don't want to alienate your neighbours or loved ones, after all... or do you?

When you set out to buy yourself an amplifier, you need to ask yourself a couple of questions, the most important of which is, 'Am I going to use an amp purely to practise with or is it likely that I am going to want to play live with a band regularly at some point?' I know I'm stressing the point a bit, but this might just be another good reason to leave buying an amp for a little while just to see where you're going with the instrument.

Essential chic – valves or transistor?

At one point in time (circa 1970) there raged a furious debate as to which was better; valve amps or transistor. Valves represented outmoded technology pretty much everywhere else and the electronics industry was busy welcoming new transistor technology with open arms. By comparison, transistors were more reliable and a more stable way of producing good clean power. Valves, like lightbulbs, had a limited lifespan and could vary tremendously in output and performance from one to the next. Surely guitarists would prefer transistors, too? Well, although as I say the debate raged for a long time, in the end guitarists voted with their wallets and continued to buy into valve amplification pretty much to a man. Why? Well, I'm going to take a deep breath here and say that they just sound better, that's all. It's the way you can get a valve amp to distort – it's far more musical than its transistor counterpart.

The scientific reasons are basically that you have to force a transistor to distort whereas a valve will do it as naturally as anything. It's slightly more involved (and hellishly more technical) than that, of course. But that's it in a nutshell.

These days the two technologies sit quite happily side by side with valves glowing away quite merrily in guitarists' amplifiers, whilst transistors do their best to deliver massive amounts of undistorted power through PA systems (about which, more in a minute).

Practice amps

By definition, a practice amp is a low-powered (transistor) affair which will allow you to hear what you're doing, add distortion and a few effects and generally enjoy all the benefits of a much larger, professional set-up, without the impracticalities of too much volume and physical size.

Today, plenty of manufacturers start their amp range with some absolutely minute, battery-powered amps costing only 50 pounds or so and, if you're dead set on hearing your new electric guitar straight away, it might be worth considering something like this. If you do decide to up-grade after a few months, you will still find plenty of occasions to use the battery-powered amp – camping, parties... you get the picture.

The next step up is a bigger, mains-operated affair which has many of the features of its bigger brothers but with reduced output and size.

We'd better say a few words about power here, because it confuses a lot of people.

Watts

Amplifiers are power-rated in watts, but we have to beware here because it's not as straightforward as it seems. Owing to some sort of mathematical hocus pocus, wattage is measured on a logarithmic scale which probably means as much to you as it does to me, but the end result is that 100 watts is only twice as *powerful* as 10 watts. So don't let anyone tell you that 50 watts is much more powerful than 30, because it's not!

Having said all this, practice amps usually weigh in at around 10, 12, 15 or 20 watts and have built-in speakers which could be eight, 10 or 12 inches in diameter. Because of the mathematical conundrum mentioned above, even at this power output, practice amps are still quite capable of rattling windows and shaking

floors and so a certain amount of restraint is called for in their use.

What sort of features do you need on a practice amp?

You can expect to find volume, treble and bass controls on an amp of pretty much any size (except, possibly, for the mini battery-powered jobs). You'll find a 'gain' control, too, which controls the amount of distortion present in the signal. It's worth coming to terms with distortion straight away; guitar players are probably the only consumers of electronic audio gear where distortion is actually welcome! It's weird that electric guitar players rely on a sound which was originally an abuse of electronics – turn the amp up until it distorts and the guitar sounds better. Doesn't really make sense, does it? But it's a fact that the electric guitar wouldn't be the same instrument any other way.

So you will probably find some sort of control to turn up the distortion on your amp (independent of the overall volume, it must be said).

You might even find reverb on some of the smaller amps. Reverb is an electric means of adding a slight delay to your signal, making it sound like you're playing in a big hall when, in fact, you're still safe in your living room. It's an effect which you'll recognise immediately when you hear it (see the chapter 'What Are Effects Units?').

You don't actually need anything else to begin with and, if you've decided that playing live is not for you, then a good practice amp will serve your needs well. If you've decided otherwise, read on...

Larger amps

To stand much of a chance of being heard in a live situation, an amp probably has to have a power output of about 30 watts at the very least. It's very likely that it will need a couple of speakers, too, although this isn't always the case. The efficiency of the electronics involved has a lot of bearing on how useful an amp is on stage; I've heard some incredibly 'loud' 30 watt and some very 'quiet' 100 watt amps and so it's not always wise to go on figures alone.

The evolution of stage amplification was a long and, for some, painful one. It was during the mid-

60s that the 100 watt 'stack' – so called because it comprised a 100 watt amp sitting atop a 'stack' of eight 12 inch speakers in two cabinets – became the popular on-stage amplification of the electric guitar's new-found aristocracy. In those days, you would see players like Eric Clapton and Jimi Hendrix standing, quite literally, in front of a wall of 100 watt stacks which would have to be turned up near to breaking point in order that the correct levels of distortion be achieved. In retrospect it was sheer madness and small wonder that many guitarists in those days suffered severe hearing problems as time went on. I've stood in front of many 100 watt amps when they've started to get angry and, believe me, it's a painful experience!

The problem was they'd got things arse about face; all the guitar's volume was on stage behind the musicians with the vocals being fed through a hopelessly under-powered PA system.

A little later on, two things happened. Amp technology improved to the point where you could drive them into distortion, but retain control over the overall output, meaning that the sound guitarists needed to achieve the desired tone and power could be realised at a much lower volume. This meant a far more comfortable on-stage experience for the musicians – although many spurned the new technology as 'bogus' and refused to change their high volume ways. These people are now, presumably, stone deaf.

The second thing to happen was that PA technology advanced to the stage whereby massive amounts of power could be available to project the on-stage sound to the audience through the use of microphones and DI. Monitoring facilities were improved to the point where musicians could hear each other loud and clear in concert. Thus on-stage volume could be reduced to present day levels where it is quite possible for band members to talk behind the singer's back without shouting at each other!

In short, it is possible to use amplification of apparently meagre output even in a stadium situation, knowing that the PA system will deliver your message to the assembled throng at a suitable trouser-flapping level.

Having said all that, when performing in smaller venues (ie pubs) it is not always practical or possible to mike everything in the band up and feed it through the PA and so your 'back line' (ie your on-stage amplification) still has to be man enough to be heard at the back.

I would still say, however, that in most cases a good, 30-50 watt amp should do the trick. Let's be careful out there!

Overall, and in conclusion, I would have to say that, armed with a reasonable guitar and amplifier, it is possible to achieve a very professional result in the playing arena. I would, once again, caution against impulse buying with the thought at the back of your mind that such-and-such a guitar/amplifier will either make the job of learning to play any easier or quicker just because it costs thousands of pounds. It won't. The only thing that will improve you as a guitarist is practice!

how many chords do I need to know?

Well, how many chords are you actually going to use? A lot of confusion in the business of learning guitar is caused by people thumbing their way through a chord book and becoming seriously depressed at the fact that there seems to be an almost endless supply of the dratted things! You'd be surprised by how many people have asked me, 'Do I have to know ALL of these?' when faced with a chord book. So many times has it happened, in fact, that I've affected a highly theatrical method of reply. Now, if someone waggles their chord book at me and demands, 'Do I have to know all these chords?' I pick up a dictionary and say, 'Do you believe that you have to know all of the words in here?'. 100% of them say no. It's the same thing. There are everyday chords, highly specialised chords, chords you'll probably only ever use once in a blue moon... and so on. The most important thing is that you learn the ones you're going to need the most (and, if you're a beginner, in the order that is easiest to grasp) and that's the nut we're going to try and crack in this chapter.

So how do we separate the wheat from the chaff – or the neat from the naff? We need a ratings table, for a start. Let's imagine that you could put every song ever written into a computer database and have the hapless machine come up with a kind of chordal league table. Well, I wish I had the resources and time, etc, but I don't and so you're going to have to bear with me on this one!

Basically you can get an awful lot of musical spadework done (I mean, you can really dig some quite impressive holes here, so listen up) with a complete set of major chords, minor chords and dominant sevenths. We're not going to worry too much about why these things are called what they're called just yet, but bear with me for now.

OK, it's maths time. There are 12 notes in the musical pot which means that there are 12 major chords, 12 minor chords and 12 dominant seventh chords. So the answer, I suppose, to the question of how many chords you need to know is '36'.

Are things really as simple as that? Well, yes, they are actually. But knowing 'only' 36 chords is going to hamper you a little in certain areas; let me explain. If you're at all familiar with some of the guitar's nastier habits, you'll be aware that there are several different places on the fretboard where you can play a single chord. In other words, you can have one chord, but plenty of different places on the fingerboard where you can play it. You may have read, too, that it's good to know at least three versions of every chord because this will aid your flexibility as a player no end – and that's very true. But, at the risk of repeating myself, you can cover an awful lot of ground with just 36 chords.

So here, I've got to sit on the fence and tell you, 'Right, here's a simple plan for you to learn all the chords you're going to need for a long time, and in the right kind of order, too...' but at the same time I have to act as tempter and seduce you into learning a few variations, as well.

In contemporary music books, chords are written down on grids like this:

example 1

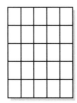

The six vertical lines represent the strings of the guitar whilst the horizontal lines represent the frets. If you imagine that your guitar is standing upright on the floor facing you, you'll see the similarity. Finger positions are marked on the strings as 'blobs' like this:

example 2

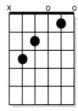

Above, we have a C major chord and the 'blobs' are telling you to put your fingers on the third fret on the A string, the second fret on the D string and the first fret on the B string. The 'x' over the bass E string is telling you not to sound that string when you play the chord, whilst the 'o' is telling you that it's OK to sound that particular 'open' string.

OK? Well, that's just for reference, now we'll look at a sensible order in which to learn chords.

Chords can be grouped together in grades of difficulty; some chords go easy on the fingers, others are quite awkward and require a little time to get used to... and others are downright pigs to come to terms with. I would say that a good 'starter pack' would look something like this:

example 3

CD Track
3

Em	D maj	C maj	D7	A7	E7	E maj

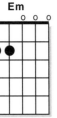 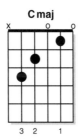 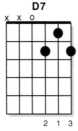 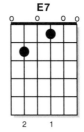 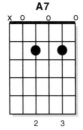 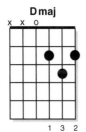 

The above chords fall into a loose 'nothing too awkward' category. When you play each of these chords, make sure that everything is ringing loud and clear by playing one string at a time, like you hear on the CD. Check for muffled notes or buzzes and adjust the position of your fingers slightly until you get a clean note. In the main, a buzz means that you're not using enough pressure (it doesn't have

to be a white-knuckled grip) or that you're playing too far away from the fret. Position your finger snugly behind the fret for the best effect. Muffled notes, on the other hand, are nearly always caused by a finger on your left hand laying gently on a string and muting it. The golden rule is to remember to use your fingertips so that they stand clear of the surrounding strings.

Once you've mastered the first set of chords, move onto the next group:

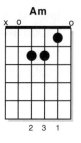

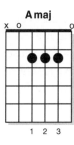

As before, check that everything is as it should be by playing each note individually. Incidentally, if this is ground that you have already covered elsewhere, then fear not – things are going to get slightly more advanced fairly soon!

The next group contains a couple of real hurdles to get across!

example 5

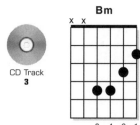

The above chords represent a bit of a challenge for a lot of guitarists and so don't become frustrated if you find that they seem impossible to begin with. Take special notice of which fingers I've recommended and persevere!

From now on, things become a little frantic. I'll give you another set of chords and then we'll talk a bit about barre chords...

example 6

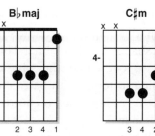
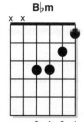
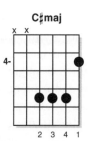

Only four this time; and you're probably wondering where the other 14 are. Well, it's my belief that the easiest way to carry on and go forward now is to learn barre chords... The chords in the above example would be a lot easier to play as barre versions, for instance. It just takes a little bit more work.

Barre chords

A barre chord is one where the first finger lays across all six strings, stopping them all. Realistically, you're not going to be able to do this right away – we're in that area where we have to allow muscles and so on to develop first. But barre chords make the job of learning a lot of variations a very easy task. Well, pretty easy, anyway...

Your first task in this area is to lay your first finger over all six strings and make sure you can get a good note out of each. A tip here is not to try and stop the strings with the flat of your finger, it's more the outer edge that has the task of holding the strings down.

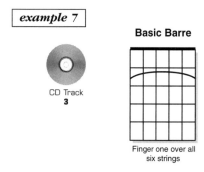

example 7

CD Track
3

Basic Barre

Finger one over all
six strings

Sound each string and make sure everything is ringing loud and clear once again. If it isn't, change the position of your finger slightly until things improve. Don't hold the position for too long because once again you can invite cramp into your life quite quickly this way.

After trying this for a few practice sessions (and you'll have to wait for part two of the book to find out how all this fits together into your very own practice schedule) try this:

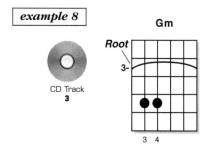

example 8

CD Track
3

Gm

Root

3-

3   4

This is, believe it or not, probably the easiest barre chord to begin with – although it may take you a little while before you agree with me on this one!

At this point, you might actually welcome some good news. You might still be wondering what the precise advantage of learning barre chords is... OK; the advantage of learning barre chords is that they're *movable*. Learn a major chord in a barre position, move it up a fret and it becomes another major chord, repeat as necessary until you've got all 12 major chords – with one shape! Now, you have to admit that this kind of thinking fits into our 'economical' guitar method – I mean, 12 chords from learning only one shape? A ratio of 12:1? This is why I implore you to overcome the physical difficulties of coming to terms with barre chords – it will give you the facility to learn chords 12 at a time from here on in.

Of course, I wasn't wasting your time by giving you all those non-barre shapes earlier. You'll still use those chords pretty much every day and a combination of the two different types is going to be a pretty tough act to beat.

Barre chord shapes

I'm going to give you two of everything here, but we're still sticking to our 'only the necessary chords' policy, don't fear! Here are the two principal barre shapes for major chords:

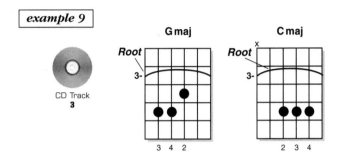

Watch the fingering here, it's important. Talking of fingering, I'll tell you of another physical requirement that the guitar asks of you. At present, the third finger of your left hand probably isn't terribly strong (unless you're left-handed and took my advice to play the 'regular way round'). What's more, the joints in that finger are quite happy as they are, bending towards your palm and so on. Well, some day soon, you're going to be able to take a shortcut into playing this chord shape:

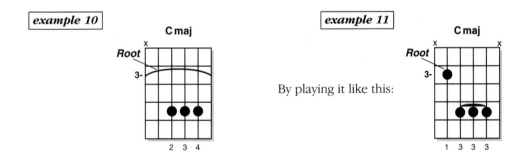

By playing it like this:

It's not really a barre chord any more – at least by definition, because the first finger doesn't extend all the way across the fretboard and you're only playing the central four strings. It may seem impossible at first and remember, you've got the other version to be going on with for now. But, in the end, this version is going to be easier and more convenient to play. Check out a couple of concert videos and if you don't see the guitarist playing this shape at least once, I'll buy you a beer next time we meet!

But, as I say, the joint at the top of your third finger, left hand is probably quite content to mind its own business; but, by practising the 'shortcut barre chord shape', it will gradually attain the flexibility required (it's a bit like ballet – well, not much, but I expect you can see what I mean). Remember, we're going against nature a bit here and so don't force things, the knack will come of its own accord and you mustn't hurry things.

Minor barre chord shapes

We've already looked at one of the principal minor barre shapes, but I just love repeating myself and so here it is again, alongside another...

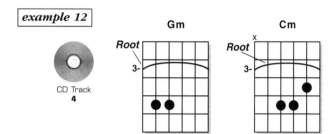

example 12

CD Track
4

As before, one is a six-string shape, the other only uses the upper five strings.

Seventh barre chord shapes

example 13

Our final pair of barre shapes covers the seventh chord type:

CD Track
4

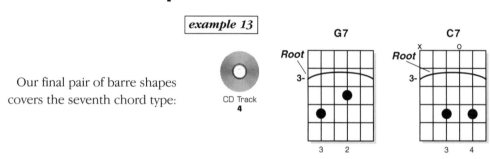

As long as you take special note of the fingering, sound each string individually to make sure you've got no unsociable buzzes or muted notes, then everything should be fine.

I will repeat that playing barre chords at first puts a strain on your left hand, particularly the muscle between the index finger and thumb. This will develop slowly and there will come a day when playing barre chords presents you will no difficulty at all. But, just like you were in training for a marathon, don't expect everything to fall into place too soon. These things take time and a little practice a day will do the trick.

So now you have quite a supply of chords at your disposal; a handful of shapes down by the guitar's nut and six barre shapes which will take you all over the fretboard. But how do we work out where to play everything? You need a neck chart and, although I'm going to provide you with one, I'd rather that you draw one out for yourself, fill in all the notes without looking at this book (I'll tell you how in a minute) and pin it up where you practise so that you see it every day. Here's the chart:

example 14

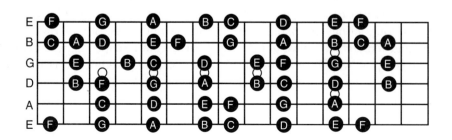

Now, you'll notice that I haven't filled in every fret. In fact what I've done is fill in all the straightforward notes like A, E, D and B and left out all the ones with names like B♭ (that's B flat) or C# (and that's called C sharp). I believe that by doing so, the chart doesn't look so cluttered. If I were to put every single note on the fingerboard – and bear in mind that some notes have two names – the information would be too dense for you to use. So let's just spend a minute or two to see exactly where the sharps and flats fit in.

First of all, here's the music alphabet which we've seen (one way or another) before:

A   B   C   D   E   F   G

All pretty straightforward – seven note names. But the full musical retinue is actually twelve notes, so let's fill in the gaps… but first, a couple of words about sharps and flats. For a very good reason (although I don't think I've ever met anyone who could tell me exactly what that very good reason is!) the notes that occur in between the magnificent seven notes shown above all have two identities. For example, there is a note between A and B, which we can call either A# (ie A 'sharp') or B♭ (ie B 'flat'). The brief and, I hope satisfactory, answer for now is that this is so the note can either be identified as 'belonging' to B

(B♭) or 'belonging' to A (ie A#). It's not the most perfect explanation, but it's going to have to do for now, otherwise we'll be here all night! (Seriously, if you crave further explanation of this and some other of music's little mysteries, you would do well to buy a book on music theory like the excellent Associated Board series, which should be able to offer in-depth insight. We've got a 'bare bones only' brief here!)

So here is the full scale, with both sharps and flats in their correct places – and this, ladies and gents, is known as the chromatic scale:

A   A#/B♭, B   C   C#/D♭, D   D#/E♭, E
F   F#/G♭, G   G#/A♭, A

Now you'll notice immediately that there isn't a sharp and flat for every note of the scale and the only way to remember this is to learn it gradually as you use it. I'll tell you how in a few paragraphs. You can probably see, as well, why I decided not to clutter the fretboard diagram with sharps and flats!

If I can refer you back to the six barre chord shapes we were looking at a moment ago, you'll notice that the 'root' note of each chord is marked. This is the note which give the chord its name – and so, if we were to take this chord shape…

example 15

CD Track
5

…and line it up with the fifth fret – where we find the note A on the bass string – we end up with A major. Move it up a few frets until the root note lines up with C (ie at the eighth fret) and you have C major. Simple, huh?

All you have to do with this system to start with is play with it. Pick a note – let's say G – and find the two major, two minor and two seventh barre chords. Play them all and then get on with

something else. Choose a different note every day and you'll soon find that you're not only getting the hang of what is a very important chord system, but you begin to get faster and faster when you set out to find a chord. That is what I call 'positive practice' and it won't be the first time this book will find me recommending that you carry out a simple manoeuvre once a day, I can assure you!

Rock chords

You may have heard of the term 'rock chords' or 'power chords' or even 'fifth chords' whilst dallying on the nursery slopes of guitar playing. These shapes play the role of principal boy in the pantomime that is rock guitar and so it's probably a good idea to look at them right here and now.

They fit quite neatly into our scheme of things because they are movable and function in exactly the same way that ordinary barre shapes do. Their other advantage is the fact that they are 'genderless'; the one shape will fit either major, minor or seventh chords. The reason why 'fifth chords' are so adaptable in this way is that they really only contain two notes as opposed to a regular chord's three. The missing note is the all-important third – the note which determines a chord's major or minor identity.

They are used quite a lot in the theatre of rock guitar and sound good when driven through an amp at Def Con 3 type levels! Let's see what they look like:

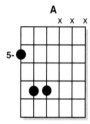
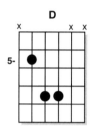

You might be able to see that these shapes are just the basic major/minor barre shapes pruned down a little.

It's definitely a good idea to come fully to terms with this shape because of its simplicity and frequency of use. Play them all over the fretboard, just to get used to moving them.

What about all the other chord shapes?

Believe it or not, what you've just learned, or are in the process of learning, will cover an amazing amount of musical ground before you need any other chord shapes. In other words, we've kept to our brief and dealt with music's hard core – but, sure, you're going to find other chords cropping up in music and you can deal with them one of about three ways:

One

You could buy a chord book and every time you come across a chord that isn't covered by the barre system we've looked at so far, look it up and learn it. But sometimes, buying a book full of about a thousand chords can be a little like opening Pandora's Box. Even if you're totally in command of all the chords we've looked at so far, you can often lose the will to live merely by trying to come to terms with the fact that there is still more to learn.

Although I wholeheartedly recommend that, at some time, every guitar student invests in a good chord book – as long as they treat it like a dictionary and not like a tutor – for now, this might be a little too fallible...

Two

You could make sure that every time you come across a chord you've never met before, you learn the barre version of it so that you save yourself some learning time in the future. (This way, you'd be learning 12 versions of every new chord and that's got to be worthwhile!) But this still relies on you having to take on board some new information all the time and there's always the danger that you'll run into that unknown chord just at the wrong time (ie when you're showing off your new-found guitar prowess to some carefully chosen young friends, or something).

Three

You can cheat. Well, it's not really cheating – it's just making the most of what you've already learned by stretching it even further. I'll explain; chords, as we have seen, split themselves into three essential groups or families. There's the major chord family, the minor chord family and the sevenths family. It might come as a pleasant surprise to learn that virtually every chord you'll ever come across belongs to one of these three families. So – if you can identify an unknown chord's family connection, you're already half way home. Why? Because nearly 99.999% of the time you can play the chord of that same family that you already know instead... that's why!

Chord families

The area that we've looked at in terms of chords is split into three: majors, minors and dominants. Now, I'm going to have to get very slightly technical here for a few moments, but I'm sure it's nothing you can't handle!

Chords are characterised principally by their 'spellings' – that is, exactly which notes of a scale are played simultaneously to make up the sound. In the main, chords usually only contain three or four notes, although, from the guitar's point of view it might be tempting to think there's more because we're used to playing six strings at once. But you'll find that there's usually one or two repeats in there, just to strengthen up the areas that need strengthening harmonically. And we give that sound a name and identify it by using a sort of 'shorthand'. Let's look at a bit of musical geography for a moment. Here's a scale:

C	D	E	F	G	A	B	C
1	2	3	4	5	6	7	1

These are the notes of the C major scale with numbers below which show any note within the scale's position. For instance, the note E is said to be C major's 'third'. Let's take another; in the key

of C major, A is the 'sixth'. You see, it's not really mysterious at all, it's plain common sense most of the time.

OK, let's look at another scale, just for good measure. Here's the scale of G major:

G	A	B	C	D	E	F#	G
1	2	3	4	5	6	7	1

So, if we wanted to find G major's 'third', it would be.... anyone? Dead right, it would be B. And the sixth? Yep, it would be E. Piece of cake, right?

So if I told you that the 'spelling' of a major chord is the first, third and fifth notes of the relevant scale played together, it would make some sort of sense. In order to really rub this little nugget of chord wisdom home, we'll look at a couple of examples: the chord of C major is made up from the first, third and fifth notes from its scale...

Scale of C:

C	D	E	F	G	A	B	C
1	2	3	4	5	6	7	1

And the chord of C major (first, third and fifth together) would be...

C	E	G
1	3	5

And, just to really throw this concept into the dirt and jump up and down on it...

Scale of G:

G	A	B	C	D	E	F	G
1	2	3	4	5	6	7	1

And therefore, the chord of G major...

G	B	D
1	3	5

It might come as something of a relief to know that I'm not going to go into why it's these three notes from a major scale which make up the staple of harmony as we know it. We'll leave that one for another time – but, if your appetite for knowledge in these matters is still not fully quenched, then I can only point you once again in the direction of any number of music theory text books! We're having much too much fun to get too technical – besides, I promised I wouldn't tell you anything I didn't think you'd ever need to know and I'm sticking to it!

Minor chords

Thankfully, minor chords are 'spelled' in exactly the same way as major chords – we've just got a different parent scale. So the chord of C minor is still the first, third and fifth notes of the scale played together – it's just the C minor scale instead of the major. I feel a diagram coming on...

C minor scale:

C	D	E♭	F	G	A♭	B♭	C
1	2	3	4	5	6	7	1

Chord of C minor:

C	E♭	G
1	3	5

You'll have noticed that despite the fact that the C minor scale is positively awash with flat signs, there's actually only one note different from the major version of the chord – E♭, (E 'flat'). Just to make sure that there's no confusion when we talk about chord spellings, we usually emphasise the difference by saying 'flat third' and writing it like this:

C	E♭	G
1	♭3	5

It's worth remembering for clarity's sake.

As before, I'll really ram this point home with another example:

Scale of A minor:

A	B	C	D	E	F	G	A
1	2	3	4	5	6	7	1

A minor chord:

A	C	E
1	♭3	5

That's where all this 'flat third' business really comes into its own; there's not necessarily going to be a flat sign by the third to remind us, it's all to do with the exact distance between the first and third notes in semitones. Look again at the chromatic scale:

C C#/D♭ D D#/E♭ E F F#/G♭ G G#/A♭ A A#/B♭ B C

If you count up how many notes there are between C and E (ignoring the 'two names for one note' situation) you'll find that there are five semitones (inclusively) in between. Now count how many there are for C to E♭ – one less, I make it. So there is a difference between the two which is very real and it doesn't matter what the note's name is, it's all to do with its physical distance from the first note in the scale. Phew!

Just to reassure you, I would say that once you've got a basic understanding of all this, you are free to take it all for granted and forget about it. You probably won't have to get involved in chord spellings or music maths – that's really only the domain of music teachers and the odd psychopath (and I'd lay odds on which of these two species can be the more dangerous!).

Dominant chords

Dominant chords are just a bit different – but not so much that it's going to cause us any real bother. The major and minor chords we've 'spelled' already are three note affairs, but the dominant chord contains four notes. The reason why has an awful lot to do with the musical job this type of chord is expected to perform. For now, just be aware that major and minor chords usually have three notes and dominants have four.

Here's a dominant scale:

C	D	E	F	G	A	B♭	C
1	2	3	4	5	6	♭7	1

You'll notice that we now have a B♭ in the scale and that I've put a flat sign before the '7' underneath. This is just to differentiate between the seventh note of a major scale and that of a the dominant variety.

The 'spelling' of a dominant chord starts off in a very familiar way:

C dominant scale:

C	D	E	F	G	A	B♭	C
1	2	3	4	5	6	♭7	1

C7 chord (aka 'C dominant 7'):

C	E	G	B♭
1	3	5	♭7

Like I said, four notes. The first three are exactly the same as the major chord, but in practice, adding the flat seventh makes an important difference.

As before, we'll look at the same thing in a different key.

G dominant scale:

G	A	B	C	D	E	F	G
1	2	3	4	5	6	♭7	1

G7 chord:

G	B	D	F
1	3	5	♭7

Remember that a flat seven is still a flat seven whether or not it is actually a 'flat' note; just like the difference between a major and minor thirds, it's down to the musical distance between the notes. Check out the chromatic scale diagram again and notice the difference between B and B♭ in terms of their distance from C.

So how does being made aware of all this fascinating stuff help you cheat your way through a song's chord arrangement? Like I said, most chords belong to one of these three families and so, if you don't know a chord, but you can identify its family

connection correctly, you simply play one you *do* know from that group. I'll show you how it works; look at these chord types:

C maj7
C6
C6(add9)
C maj 9

And now let's look at their spellings:

C maj 7 = C E G B
C6 = C E G A
C6(add9) = C E G A D
C maj 9 = C E G B D

Notice the similarity? They all contain the basic major chord spelling of C, E and G. And so, if you came across one of the above chords and didn't know it, you could play the straightforward major version and all would be well. After all, what's your alternative? Play a wrong chord, or play nothing at all? Both would be inappropriate (although playing nothing at all is probably going to do the least harm in one way). By substituting a chord you *do* know for one of a similar type you can't possibly be going wrong. In fact, if you've committed any crime against music at all, it's just that you haven't played enough notes in the chord – but you've certainly played the important ones!

In short, the major family will usually identify themselves by either having 'maj' or 'major' in the title, the only exception being 'sixth' chords. Usually, you'll just see G6 or E6, but you can take it for granted that they're major because they would have to tell you otherwise (ie you might see 'minor sixth').

The minor chord family will always give itself away by saying 'minor' somewhere in the title. As an example:

C min6
C min7
C min 9

As I hope I've made clear, the difference in music between major and minor is almost as significant as the difference between male and female – and we all know how important that is. That's why it's so vital that you never confuse the two and play a major instead of a minor or vice versa – so stay sharp. Oh, you probably want proof that the magic still works with the minor family:

C min6 = C E♭ G A
C min7 = C E♭ G B♭
C min9 = C E♭ G B♭ D

Once again, the common denominator is the minor chord and you can safely play that instead of the above chords – you'll *always* be right.

The dominant family

Arguably, the dominant family is by far the most expansive, although it depends on what style of music you're playing as to the exact 'seventh saturation' factor. Jazz, for instance, is riddled with the things...

Dominant chords will quite often turn up in their normal guise – they're four-note chords and, as a chord grows it generally becomes less readily useful. If you put too many notes in a chord, it would sound like someone sitting on a piano. Like so many things, it's not the size of the chord, it's what you do with it that counts...

But you will see chords like these:

C9
C13

And if you still don't trust me...

C9 = C E G B♭ D
C13 = C E G B♭ D A

You can see that the basic seventh we already dealt with miles back at the beginning of this chapter will do quite nicely and I'll bet nobody notices.

But seventh chords do have one nasty habit that's worth mentioning; not content with having more members of their parent scale included over and above the basic 1 3 5 ♭7, they also quite often include the chromatic tones, too. This is where you get some of the really scary-looking stuff from. You'll find chords like these:

C7#9
C7♭9
C13♭9

But once again...

C7#9 = C E G B♭ E♭
C7♭9 = C E G B♭ D♭
C13♭9 = C E G B♭ D♭ A

The theory holds up. Now let me say at this point that this kind of chord is relatively unusual and not something you're going to come across every time you sit down with some music. These are very highly 'coloured' chords which are included within a song's framework to achieve a specific effect. You definitely won't find an 'altered seventh' (as they are called) lasting very long in a regular piece of music. So, in other words, you can play a normal seventh quite happily in the knowledge that you're well and truly in the chordal ball park! What's more, you'll soon come to recognise and learn the ones which crop up the most.

Exceptions to the rule

You were just waiting for me to say that the system isn't 100% weren't you...

In this chapter, we've looked at things in the order of importance; first, we got you playing some basic chord shapes and then, by looking at the barre chord system, we developed a means of spreading our chord knowledge all over the fretboard. Then, we looked at a system where we could make the fullest possible use of what we'd learned without having to take on board too much more information. It's a good system and it's got me personally out of trouble on a number of playing occasions! But there are just a few chords that need to be watched out for...

Diminished and augmented chords

No matter how perfect, bomb-proof or watertight a system appears to be, there's always going to be at least one exception to the rule. In the case of chords and this system in particular, there are actually two exceptions – the diminished and augmented chord. They don't fit into our neat little world because their construction is so unique that neither of them can be readily replaced by anything else.

We've seen that chords belong to one of three family groups and that, as long as you recognise the family ties, you can make effective substitutions within each group – OK? Check back, and you'll remember that the magic worked because the actual core of the chord remains constant. I'm afraid that this is just not so for the last two chord types. But it's not all bad news, as we'll see in a minute.

You'll remember that the difference between major and minor chords is down to the third – whether it's flat or natural:

Major chords:

1 3 5

Minor chords:

1 ♭3 5

Even the dominant family looks pretty familiar when we break it down:

Dominant chords:

1 3 5 ♭7

The one great consistency with all these chords so far is that, whatever the third is doing, the fifth is always the same. Enter the diminished and augmented chords! Here's a diminished triad:

1 ♭3 ♭5

And here's an augmented triad:

1 3 #5

You could say that the diminished triad is minor

with a flattened fifth and that the augmented is a major with a sharp fifth. So distinct is the sound of both of these triads, that in either case, nothing that we've looked at will really do instead.

At this point, you probably need the good news and I've got lots of it! For one, both of these chords, because of their dissonant nature, are fairly unusual. (In fact, you're fairly safe to think of them as 'special effect' chords.) Secondly, there is really only one shape each to learn for both – yes, really!

In actual use, you're more likely to see a four note construction for either the augmented or diminished chord and they are both likely to be referred to as 'sevenths', too. So, just for the record, here are the grisly details...

C diminished 7:

C E♭ G♭ A
1 ♭3 ♭5 ♭♭7

C augmented 7:

C E G# B♭

You'll notice immediately that there are two flat signs before the seventh in the diminished chord and there's a really good, logical reason why and it's all to do with the nature of chord construction and the alchemy of music in general – but you don't have to be bothered about it. Basically, the third has been flattened by one semitone and so has the fifth – so why not affect the seventh in exactly the same way, too? In polite conversation, a '♭♭7' can safely be referred to as a 'double flat seventh' without offending anyone unduly.

So what about some chord shapes? Firstly, here's an all-purpose diminished chord shape:

example 16

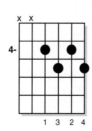

CD Track
5

Why 'all-purpose'? Because every diminished chord can be used in four ways. The above diminished chord is C diminished (or 'dim' for short) – but it's also E♭ dim, G♭ dim and A dim too. I won't go into detail as to exactly why, just trust me on this one! So, if you know this one shape and can play it in three different locations on the fretboard, you know every diminished chord there is. In other words, a diminished chord can be called after any note within it, which makes it quite an economic little entity, to my mind!

But does the same sort of magic apply to augmented chords, too? Yep; no problem. Gather round...

The basic triad (ie C E G#) can be played thus:

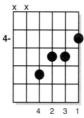

CD Track
5

Once again, it can be called after any note it contains and so the above chord can be called C augmented (or 'aug' for short), E aug or G# aug. Because the chord contains only three notes this time, though it means that you need to play this shape in four different places on the fretboard before you can tell yourself that you've run the augmented gamut.

We fall down a bit when we add the seventh to the augmented chord and get this shape:

CD Track
5

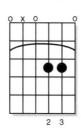

The symmetry that we relied on is no longer present and so you need to play this chord like you would a barre chord and check out where the root is and so on. But, like a barre chord, it's still only one shape to remember for 12 chords.

Once again I'll repeat that we've run through this chapter on chords in such an order that you've run into the rarest chords last – keeping in mind the lean burn brief of this book. You will come across both diminished and augmented chords

and, armed with the above information, you'll be able to deal with them with the absolute minimum fuss and effort.

That's enough about chords for now – you'll find this system works for most eventualities and that you learn more as you go along.

We'll look at how you embroider all this information on your brain in part two. But for now, let's look at something else...

do I have to learn to read music?

Heavens no! But learning tablature is a really smart thing to do. If you want to learn to read music, I'll write you another book, but for now, let's look at a form of communicating music for the guitar which pre-dates Bach...

Seriously, my philosophy regarding reading music is that I think it's important – but only if you're going to be in a situation whereby it's vital that you be able to read it. That would be if you intended to go into session work (and even then reading is far from obligatory, believe me) or pit work (that's playing in a band who play for theatre productions – not coalmining...). But if you're not going to be in that kind of position, then no, it's not so important.

Let's look at the facts; if you want to buy a music book and play the music inside, it's quite likely that the rhythm part will be covered quite adequately by chord boxes and a little bit of instinctive imagination on your part. So what about the guitar solo or melody part? Well, the chances are that it is going to be notated in tablature. If you haven't come across tablature (or 'tab' for short) before, I'll explain.

A long time ago, around the 16th century, music for guitar (or more commonly) the lute was written in a completely different and dedicated manner. The idea was that there were six lines instead of music's regular five and each of the six represented one of the instrument's strings:

example 1

The six lines represented the six strings of the guitar and carried information regarding how to play the piece in question. Tab's only drawback was that it was, as I've said, dedicated to the guitar and *only* the guitar; it wasn't possible to communicate this way with other instruments

and so tab fell out of fashion.

To cut 400 years' worth of story short, tab was revived in the 20th century as a convenient method for notating guitar music to a largely non-reading player base. It's been revised since the early days and is now both easy to use and widely accepted by music publishers world-wide. Why? Isn't it a cop-out? No! It's really useful; you've got six lines, which represent the six strings as before, but today, we put numbers on the lines to represent the frets where you are expected to play the notes concerned. A figure '0' represents an open string. And so, you might see something like this:

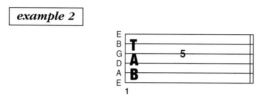

example 2

The above example means that you are expected to play the fifth note on the G string (which is the note C, if you're interested). So, if you were expected to play a whole series of notes, you might see something like this:

example 3

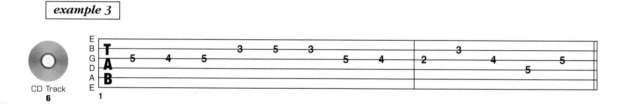

CD Track
6

Looks a little trickier, doesn't it? But you have to admit it's an awful lot easier to cope with and far more immediate than if I'd written that particular example like this:

example 4

Indecipherable at first sight, right? Although, with only the briefest explanation, most people could make some sort of sense out of the tab version. I'll add here the statistic that I usually find I can get someone reading tab in a single lesson, whereas reading music to the same sort of level takes about a year. Which one would you choose?

If you want to go the whole distance and learn to read music later on, then fine. But for now, I would encourage, cajole and generally implore you to master tablature – you're going to need it in this book and so I'm not leaving you an awful lot of choice!

Tablature's only shortfall is that it doesn't contain any rhythmic information and so playing something you've never heard before can be a bit of a hit and miss affair. But we can take for granted that most people will want to play something they've heard on record and so finding where to play the notes on the fretboard is most of the job done, the rhythm you can get from the record. Failing this, if you're the sort of adventurous type who enjoys a challenge and want to buy music you've never heard to play on the guitar and want to learn how to decipher rhythmic notation, I happen to have written another book which should serve you adequately enough! (It's called *Rhythm* and it's available through Sanctuary Publishing – just ask in the same bookshop you bought this book from!) OK – shameless advert over...

So is reading tab really as simple as all that? No other catches? No – it really is that simple and I'd recommend that you take a little time to become familiar with it (it should take you all of an hour to start feeling comfortable). Just to ensure that the tab experience is reaching you loud and clear, here are a few examples which are yours to work out and check with the CD to see if you're right.

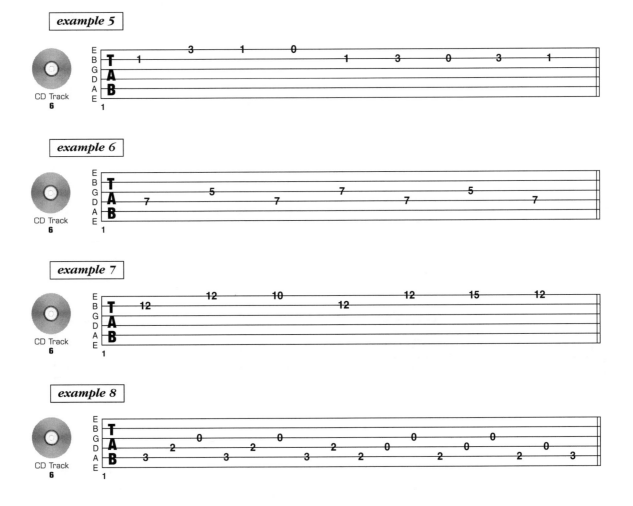

Now that wasn't so bad was it?

example 9

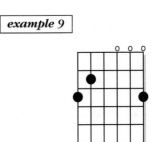

We've already seen how chords are written down on special grids or 'boxes' and are quite easy to read, but surely chords must crop up in tab, too? Yes they do and, while they might look a little like advanced mathematics to start with – certainly more complex than reading single notes – they are quite easy to come to terms with, too.

Let's take a G major chord in its regular 'box' format:

Look familiar? Right, well let's look at how the exact same information would look like in tab:

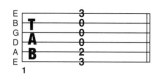

Read it from the bottom: third fret bottom string, second fret fifth string, open D, G and B strings and then the third fret on the top E string. G major.

Many guitar students back away a little when we start writing chords in tab and it does look a little daunting at first, I suppose, but it's worth persevering because it turns the system into a universal one... well, nearly.

Just to give you a bit of practice, here are some chords written down in tab format with some blank chord boxes by the side. Spend a little time converting one to the other and you'll soon start getting the hang of things.

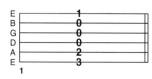

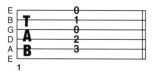

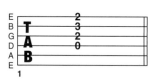
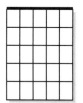

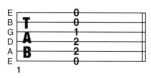
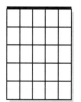
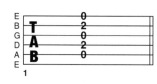
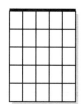

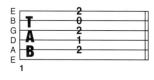
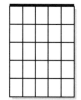
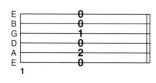
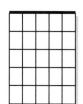

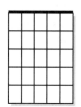

hey, how do I use one of these pick things?

With the exception of classical guitar and acoustic fingerstyle, it is customary to use a pick or plectrum to actually strike the strings on the guitar. It's the cheapest piece of gear you will ever buy yourself, costing only a few pence each, and often underestimated as having any effect on your tone or general performance. Not so! Although a good sound is down to a successful combination of many different factors, the actual method you use to pick the strings has to be of considerable importance.

Plectrums come in all shapes, sizes and thicknesses and, in my opinion, should never be taken for granted. I'll give you an example; I had a pupil once who was having a great deal of trouble playing 'cleanly' (ie without mistakes) above a certain speed. It frustrated the heck out of him, and I was quite dismayed because I couldn't see any reason why he should be having the trouble he was. His technique was otherwise fine. During one lesson, and I admit I was clutching at straws a bit here, I asked to look at his pick. He showed me and I thought it was a little on the large side and so I lent him one of mine. It worked; a few pence worth of plastic was all that had been standing in his way and from then on his picking was cleaner and more accurate than before.

Based on the experience above, I would advise everyone to buy themselves a selection of picks and spend a while experimenting with them until they find one that just 'feels' right. It's probably a good idea to repeat the experiment every so often – your playing approach will change as you learn more and different strokes might just be called for.

Rock players tend to gravitate towards heavier plectrums and by heavier I mean around .75mm to 1.00mm thick and beyond. (Plectrums are one of the only items of guitar-related hardware to have gone metric, you'll notice!) But by all means experiment; rock guitar icon Edward Van Halen uses quite a light gauge pick for a heavy rock player and so you never can tell!

The expression 'different strokes for different folks' might apply in other walks of life, but as far a guitar players in my flock are concerned there's one basic rule to begin with... and only one. It's called 'alternate picking' and you're going to hear an awful lot more about it, particularly when we reach boot camp in part two.

Simply put, it means that when you play a note on the guitar holding the pick above the string, plucking it and following through, alternate picking makes use of the upward movement you need to get back to where you started. If this action is repeated over and over, you'll find that you've got an economical picking regime which has the added benefits of being organised and predictable, too. It works both ways, of course; if you were to start playing with an upstroke of the plectrum, your next would be a downstroke and so on.

But let's not run away with ourselves too fast; a lot of people have difficulty holding a pick, let alone using one! Basically, there are no hard and fast rules to holding picks – I've seen the most amazing things work. But, I figure that if I tell you what the majority of guitar players do with their picks, you'll be on reasonably solid ground from the start.

If until now handling your plectrum has been rather a haphazard, random affair then it's fair to say that you're going to have to start off from day one again and get into the habit of applying alternate picking to everything you do. It doesn't take too long and it will help you progress on the instrument and so the necessary investment of time and patience is well worth the trouble.

We're only really interested in getting you on the starting grid in this chapter, too. Exercises to improve and render your picking technique more accurate are all part of the 10 minutes a day workout – but, for now, you just need somewhere to start.

The best place to begin alternate picking is on a single open string. It doesn't exactly sound great, but it's a way of focusing your attention on this single technique. You can use a different string every time you do the exercise – in fact this will get the hand used to being in place above all the strings and not just stuck in one position.

Start slowly – very slowly to begin with and build up speed over a number of days. Don't run away with it, though; speeding up too much too soon will only end up with inaccurate picking and, like all good board games, you'll have to return to the start and wait to throw another six!

Just for the heck of it, here's a CD example of what I mean:

example 1

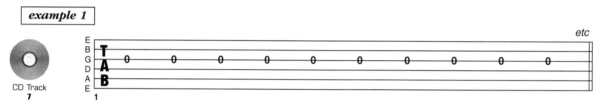

Not the most riveting piece of guitar playing, but it serves its purpose! Once you can do the above exercise evenly, fairly fast and, most importantly, without making any mistakes, move on to two strings.

example 2

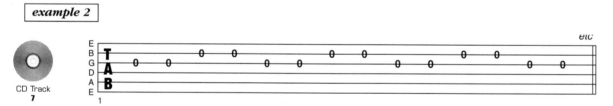

This gets you used to the next problem which is feeling confident with alternate picking whilst you change from one string to another. Once again, don't stick to a single pair of strings, change things around all the time to get you used to picking across any pair of strings.

Next, we'll try the exercise on three strings:

example 3

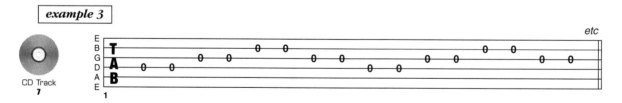

It's still not the most interesting thing to play, but it will work its magic after a while if you let it.

After only a little time, alternate picking is going to feel quite natural and you won't even have to think about it. The next few stages all feature playing scale exercises and I've covered those later on and so I won't repeat myself here.

I will mention a couple of other approaches to the fairly fundamental question of striking the strings, though...

Fingerstyle

This is a technique which acoustic players tend to use. That's an almighty generalisation, of course; there are plenty of acoustic players who play with picks. But a lot of them play with their fingers, it has to be said.

Obviously, there are advantages and drawbacks to both methods of playing. Using a pick means that it's difficult to get this kind of thing happening:

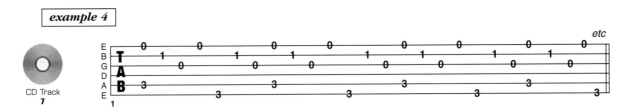

example 4

CD Track
7

Did I say difficult? I meant almost impossible! But using your fingers means you won't quite have the attack that a pick gives you. (This last fact is based on the simple notion that 1mm of plastic is going to make more of an impact on the string than soft flesh or thin fingernail. You can be far more violent with a plectrum than you'd ever dream of being with your fingers.)

Then there's the question of speed, too. Without a pick and a sensible, well-honed alternate picking regime, playing fast-ish scale passages is virtually out of the question.

Many players find that one way works for them, others do a bit of both (covering as many bases as possible, it seems, is almost universally a good idea).

If you want to explore a fingerstyle approach to playing as an alternative to using a pick, there are a few simple rules to acknowledge in this area, too.

In general, fingerstyle calls for the use of the right hand thumb, index, middle and ring fingers. The thumb tends to take care of the three 'bass'

strings (E, A and D) whilst the index, middle and ring fingers look after the G, B and E strings respectively. Now this is by no means written in stone and of course there will be times when you're doing things very differently from the way I just mentioned. The important thing is that it's a way of starting – a good discipline to kick off with. I was always told, when I was having classical guitar lessons, that I could do whatever I liked once I could actually play; until then, the deal was that I shut up and obeyed the rules! It paid off; by learning the rules, I found creative ways to break them later on...

So, if you want to begin playing fingerstyle, what's the best way of going about it? To begin with, getting the fingers used to where they are and what they're doing is the first nut to crack. The method is pretty much the same as before; a boring right hand exercise which will mean you can focus all your efforts on the fingers of one hand without anything to unnecessarily distract you.

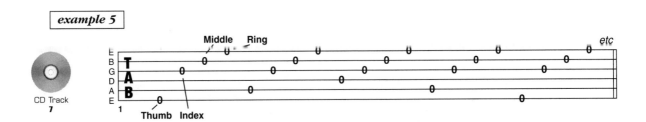

example 5

CD Track
7

When you've got all the actions of the right hand properly sorted, pick any six string chord (E or G major are good ones) and use the same plucking motion described above. It will sound a bit more

musical and possibly show you what sort of thing you do with this style of playing. If you want to explore fingerstyle technique further, then there are books which deal with the style – and studying different fingering patterns could take their place in your workout. There is obviously a fair amount of muscular development and co-ordination to be established in this department, too.

Electric fingerstyle

But do fingerstyle techniques transfer onto electric guitar? There are players who use their fingers rather than a pick. The legendary Jeff Beck, for instance, uses his fingers – as does Mark Knopfler. Both have found ways round the apparent limitations of 'electric fingerstyle' I mentioned above and neither could be said to have suffered from it. But they do represent a minority and I'm really only looking at this particular area of playing for the sake of being 'complete'.

Hybrid picking

More common than using fingers exclusively on electric guitar is a thing called 'hybrid picking'. This involves using a combination of pick and fingers – or a thumbpick and fingers – to pluck the strings. In many ways, I suppose it represents a 'best of both worlds' approach; you've got the pick there if you need the attack, and you can bring in the fingers when you want to introduce a bit of quasi-fingerstyle into a song, too.

If you want my advice on picking, though, it's this. Try alternate picking first; it's by far the most popular method for playing and it follows that the majority of people who come new to the instrument are going to get along with it. Later on, if you begin to establish your own style, you may want to try using hybrid picking, or even do away with your plectrum altogether and come up with another variation on the picking theme.

Although it's as important as any technique to begin with, later on which method you adopt to strike the strings is about as important as knowing what kind of pencil Leonardo Da Vinci used to draw *The Last Supper*. It's the end result that makes the difference.

why do I have to know scales?

I've mentioned before how learning to play any instrument is a combination of forces; that of overcoming the physical barriers any instrument puts in your way by learning co-ordination skills and developing muscles, and learning a musical vocabulary. If you remember, I compared it to learning to type on the one hand and having something to say on the other. Well, nowhere do these forces come together more readily than in the learning and practising of scales. Now, before *you* say it, let me...

Practising scales is boring...

I know! When I was nine years old I had piano lessons and my teacher made me play scales endlessly, but he never told me why. Never in such a way that a nine-year-old could understand it, anyway. But when I started to teach guitar, I realised how important the whole scale system is; it teaches co-ordination, it develops muscles – the right muscles, too – and it develops the ear. Scales therefore tie the knot between these two important areas – physical and musical development...

But they're still boring...

I know! And so what I'm going to do is make a deal with you. If I promise to teach you only the scales that you're definitely going to need and try to make learning them fun and guarantee that we'll cover as much ground with minimum effort, will you give it a try? Remember, we're going to blend all this together into a ten-minute-a-day practice routine in part two of this book and so it's not going to take up an enormous amount of your life!

OK, so how many scales do I need to know?

There are at least two answers to that question and so, at the risk of sounding like a member of Parliament squirming in front of a direct question from a political journalist, I'm craving your indulgence a bit here. It's OK, I think you win in the end!

I could answer the question one way by saying, 'You only need two scales...' and I wouldn't be lying. It's just that there are a few subdivisions of the two. Let me explain by way of a few facts.

Most music is drawn from a single musical scale which is called the major scale. It's the scale upon which everything like nursery rhymes, folk songs, pop songs to major classical works is based (generally speaking, anyway). So if it's that important, and if I also told you that about 85% of all pop, rock, country and jazz songs are based on it, you'd agree that it was probably important to learn it – right? Or at least learn how it *sounds* – remember, you'll be introducing your ear to a major part of music's vocabulary by doing so.

At this point, it might be good to hear what the major scale sounds like on a guitar:

example 1

C MAJOR SCALE

CD Track
8

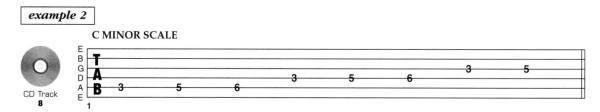

Nothing too controversial there, I think you'll agree. In fact, if anyone ever had a music lesson in their life (and, if it was at school, managed to stay awake during it) they will have encountered that series of notes. It's common to all music and all musical instruments, after all.

So, if the major scale is responsible for around 85% of all known pop songs, what goes on for the other 15%? Another principal force in the way that music sounds is the yin to the major scale's yang – the minor scale and, basically, it sounds like this:

example 2

C MINOR SCALE

CD Track
8

It's sadder, more forlorn-sounding than the major scale. See what I mean about yin and yang? But why did I say 'basically' just a moment ago? Well, whereas there is a single, definitive major scale, there are three minors. Sorry.

The reason for this unreasonable behaviour is a complex theoretical issue and I will try to sum it up by saying this. When music started to evolve, scale-wise it was a bit of a mess. Around the 16th century, the composers of the time agreed to sort things out so everyone knew exactly where they were. They agreed upon a single definition for the major scale – the principal scale in music even then – but when it came round to deciding which minor scale would take poll position, they must have adjourned and never really re-convened!

So where does that leave us? Well, we have to examine the territory – after all, in some cases what goes on in Symphony Hall is a bit different from what goes on at Wembley Arena, if you see what I mean.

So, for the most part, you're only going to need one minor scale – and that's the one you heard in

the last example. Just be aware that there are others – OK?

Pentatonics

I've always found it an interesting fact that, as language developed on the planet on independent continents – that is to say that all the different variations on the 'early man' theme saw the necessity to communicate and did something about it – so did music. Every culture on earth includes music as an important part of its heritage – independent of each other. But, in the same way that speech contains a few common denominators between languages, so does music and one of these is the Pentatonic scale.

A Pentatonic scale contains five notes as opposed to the two scales we've already looked at, which contain seven apiece. In fact, each of the scales we've looked at *contains* the notes of the Pentatonic scale. That is to say, the major scale contains the major Pentatonic and the minor scale contains the minor Pentatonic. Listen to this:

example 3

C MAJOR SCALE

CD Track
8

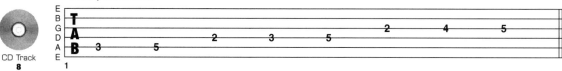

That's the major scale again – now listen to the major Pentatonicentatonic:

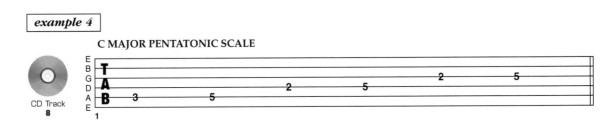

Can you hear how similar they sound? Now, here's the minor scale:

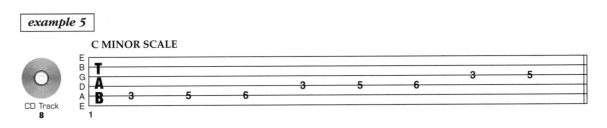

And here's the minor Pentatonic:

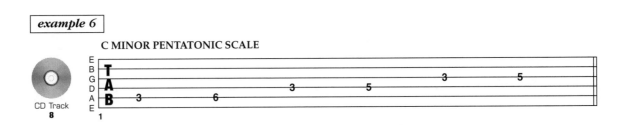

Once again, you'd have to agree that they sound fairly similar. So why do you need to know Pentatonic scales as a separate entity? Let's examine another piece of music history. I've already said that independent cultures across the musical world have got a type of Pentatonic scale as a fundamental element in their ancestry – and we're going way back here. There is evidence that even Egyptian culture thousands of years ago had a Pentatonic scale – I gather they've found instruments in pyramids and a bit of detective work into how they were tuned revealed this fact.

The role that the Pentatonic plays is the same in pretty much every case – it's a 'folk' scale. That is to say that it's not an academic scale at all, it exists primarily in 'simple' music.

It's true to say that the similarities between differently evolved Pentatonic scales are based primarily on the fact that each has five notes – but there are other similarities, too. Needless to say, we haven't got the space here for a full music treatise on pentatonics (you'll be relieved to know), but forgive me if I point out a couple of things along the way.

So how are we going to do this?

Well, you know my ethos – the most important scale takes priority and then we'll deal with the rest in order of importance.

Without any doubt, the most important scale to become fully familiar with on the guitar is the minor Pentatonic. After that, I would suggest the major scale, minor scale and finally the major Pentatonic. Four scales which will cover an incredible amount of musical ground before you need call on anything else. We will be looking at how the minor Pentatonic transforms itself into the blues scale as well, but most people agree that they are virtually the same. Well, virtually.

If you've read the chapter on chords, you might just have thought to yourself, 'Hang on; does this mean I've got to learn these four scales in every key?' Well, it has to be said that, if you're going to get the most out of your knowledge on guitar, becoming familiar with all the different keys is pretty much vitally important. But remember the barre chords? One shape, 12 applications? It's the same for the scales; you only really have to learn the various shapes once (and how they move over the neck from key to key) and you're home and dry.

The other thing is that we've got to learn the scales all over the neck – not just in one place. Now this might sound like a serious undertaking and tons of work, but, having taught this system countless times, I've never known it fail. I'll offer a little light at the end of the scale-learning tunnel: as you become familiar with the various scale shapes on the fretboard, it gets easier and easier to move them around into different keys. And yes, I'm going to tell you which order to learn them in terms of key, too. I'm sticking to the brief I set myself which is no useless information and everything in the order of importance!

The minor Pentatonic

This scale is probably the most important in rock'n'roll and all associated styles. It's bluesy and rocky and you'd have to be something pretty unusual never to need it! Let's just remind ourselves what it sounds like:

example 7

C MINOR PENTATONIC SCALE

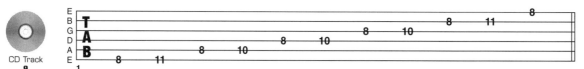

CD Track
9

Now let's hear it in context:

example 8
audio only

CD Track
8

Sound familiar? The above example wouldn't sound out of place in any blues/rock situation and might have given you some idea already as to the usefulness of the minor Pentatonic. So let's see what

it looks like on the fretboard; I'm going to write the scale out in tab and let you look at it like a chord box diagram. I find the latter a more immediate and helpful way to memorise this particular scale:

example 9

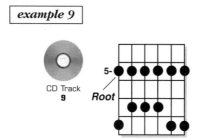

CD Track
9

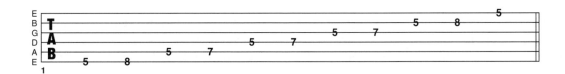

This is the minor Pentatonic scale in the key of A. Why A? Well, if we were looking for rock'n'roll's most common key, the keys of E and A would be battling it out somewhere – and I always declare A the winner. To be absolutely honest, this one shape alone offers you almost unlimited mileage on the guitar. It is, without doubt, the shape which is the most used as far as solos or melody passages are concerned, so learn it well.

But, if you study the diagram, you'll see that this particular shape in A only takes care of a relatively small chunk of neck. To be precise, it looks after the fifth to eighth frets and one look at the fretboard will tell you that there is a lot more ground to cover. The good news here is that it's probably not quite as much as you think; Ex 9 will repeat itself at fret 17. After the 12th fret, everything starts again – check out the diagram you drew out for the chapter on chords and you'll see what I mean.

There are four more shapes for the minor Pentatonic to learn – and here they are:

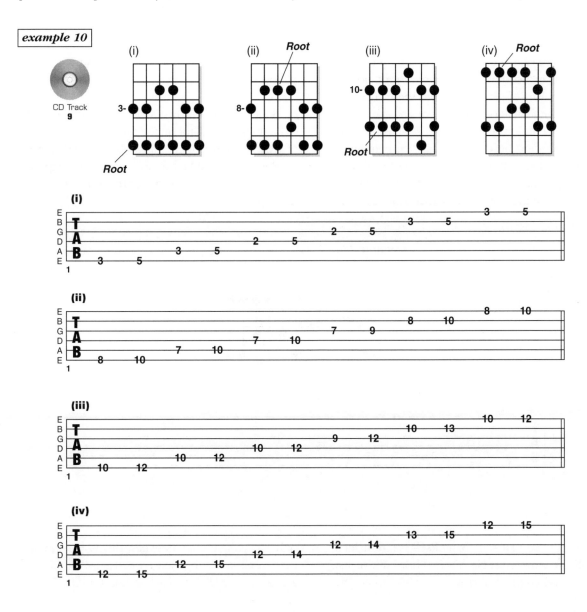

Now, you'll see that I've marked all the root notes, just like we did for the barre chords. This is very important, because this is the way you'll learn to move or 'transpose' all these shapes into the different keys. It's also important to play them through in the right way, too. Listen to this:

example 11

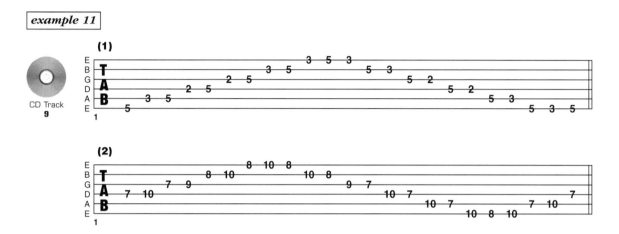

CD Track
9

Playing the scale the way I have done in Ex 11 leaves you in no doubt as to which root note it belongs to. Part of playing through these shapes is processing information for your ear and one of the most important jobs you can do is establish a sense of key in your head. As far as ear-training is concerned, it's vital and so I'm going to ask that you always practise scales this way. There's no harm in really ramming home this information, as far as

your musical ear is concerned. Believe me, you'll be lost without it!

So let's make our first key change. You're going to be doing a lot of this in the future and so it will be of great assistance to get things absolutely clear now.

Remember the first minor Pentatonic shape we looked at? Here it is again, but this time, it's in the key of G minor.

example 12

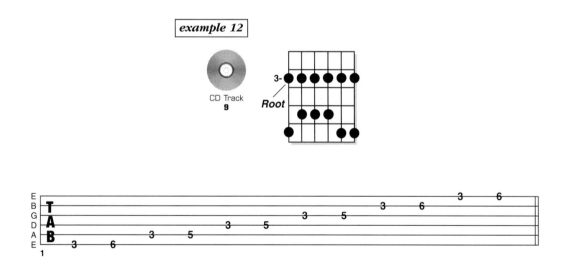

CD Track
9

Root

Now you'll see that the shape itself has remained exactly the same – just like a barre chord. We've just moved it down the fretboard a couple of frets. The

only slight difference between this G version and the A version we originally looked at is that the frets are every so slightly farther apart in G. It's an incredibly subtle difference, but you're going to notice it more and more as we move the shapes around. Eventually it will be simplicity itself to play in any key you're called upon to perform – for now, you might find that you're making a few silly mistakes.

Here are the other positions of the minor Pentatonic in G minor:

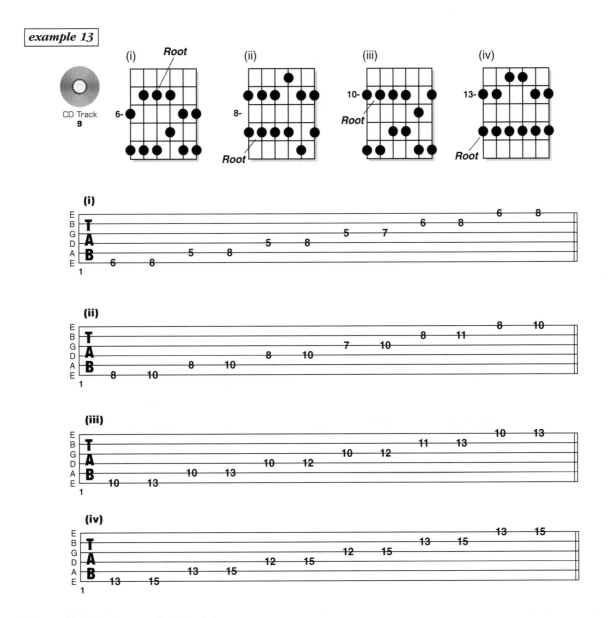

example 13

CD Track
9

If you play through these shapes again, you'll find that they might feel slightly unfamiliar merely because they are in a different place on the fretboard. The eyes and fingers are confused; despite the fact that they know these shapes fairly well, moving them causes confusion. I once spoke to a very well known jazz player who said he found it really difficult to play in the key of C because his favourite key was D♭, and if he looked down at the

fretboard whilst playing in the key of C, it looked wrong! (This was due to the fact that these two particular keys are next door neighbours – only one fret apart.)

We're going to try and make sure that we become equally familiar with all the common keys so that kind of thing doesn't happen to us. If you need another cautionary tale, when I was learning guitar, I played through the minor Pentatonic religiously every day, but always in A minor. If I had to play in any other key, I couldn't play half as well because I'd lost all my essential fretboard landmarks.

I apologise for really being a bit too obvious about this, but here's that first position once again, this time in the key of C:

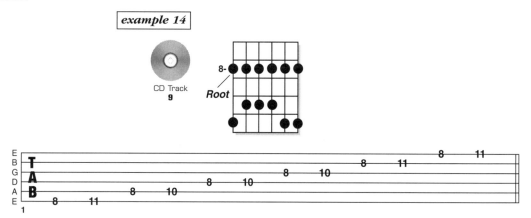

example 14

CD Track 9

Root

Make sure you understand how the system for moving the scale shapes around works; you're just lining up the root notes exactly the same way as

you did for the barre chords. That's really all there is to it. Just in case you could use another example, here's all the other shapes in the key of C minor:

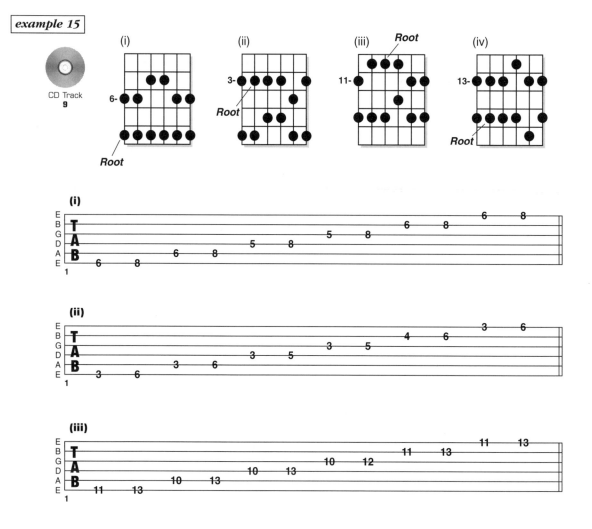

example 15

CD Track 9

(i)   (ii)   (iii)   Root   (iv)

Root   Root

Root

Root

(i)

(ii)

(iii)

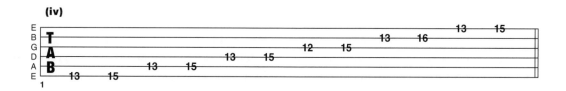

Part two of the book will give you a methodical system for learning all the various keys as part of your own DIY workout programme. As far as we're concerned, we'll get on with the next scale.

The major scale

This scale is your next priority. You may be wondering why, seeing as I said little earlier on that this is the most important scale in music, we're leaving it until now to look at it. It's true to say that it is, beyond doubt, music's most important scalar citizen – but the nature of rock music (and I use the word 'rock' as a massive umbrella term) is such that blues, which is predominately minor in nature, permeates rock music to the nth degree. The minor Pentatonic is not everything you need to know about playing blues by a long way, but it gets you far enough into the ball park for now. We'll look at adjustments a little later on when you're more used to scales.

So. The major scale, then. This time, instead of A being our default key, we're going to look at C major. C has a reputation in music for being the easiest key to come to terms with in a theoretical sense and who am I to argue? C it is, then...

Unlike the Pentatonic scale, there isn't really a 'most commonly used' version of the major scale. So we'll look at everything in order, starting at the lowest point on the guitar neck which doesn't mean that we've got to use any open strings. The reason for that is that we want all these shapes to be movable – we can work out where the open strings fit in later on.

Here's the first shape:

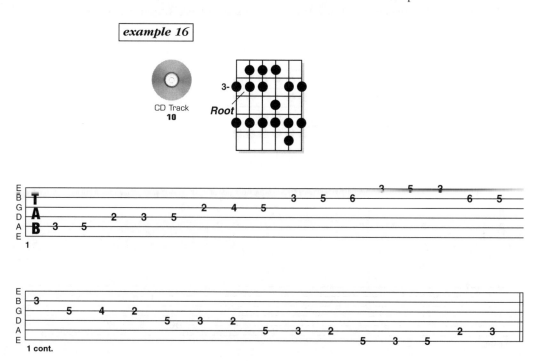

example 16

CD Track
10

Root

Once again, it's vitally important that you play the scale as you hear it on the CD. The ear has got to have a root or key note to relate all the other notes to and you'll be saving yourself a lot of time later on if both your hands and ears decide to get involved in playing scales from the word go.

Just like with the Pentatonic scales, there are five major scale shapes to learn and they fit together on the fretboard like a jigsaw puzzle. Here's the next one:

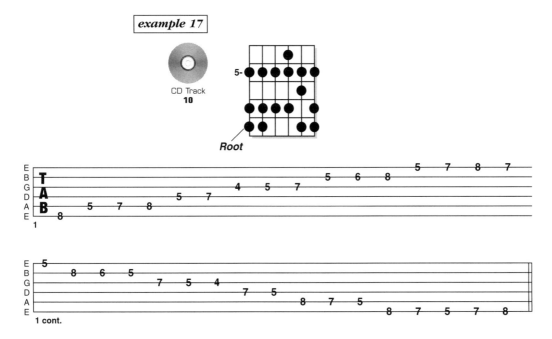

Look closely at the notes at the top of the diagram – they are the same as the ones at the bottom of the previous one. See what I mean about jigsaw puzzles? Here's the next shape:

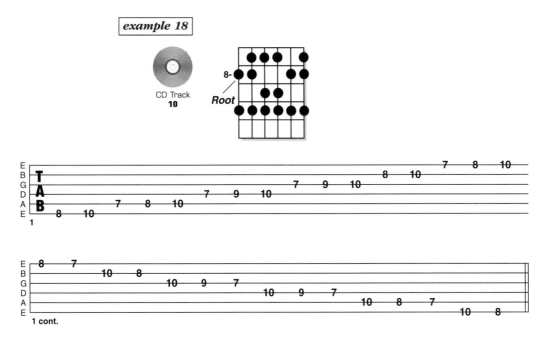

Exactly the same principle as before; begin and end on the root or key note to help your ear establish a musical sense of gravity. The next position looks like this:

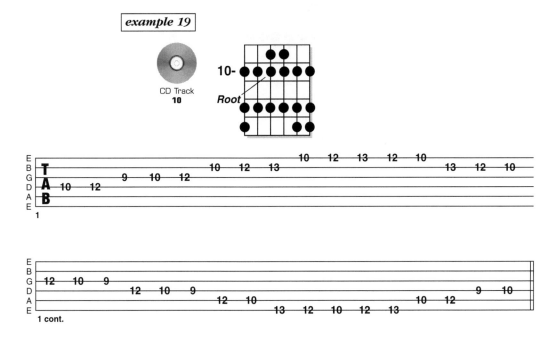

One more to go before we find that we're beginning to repeat ourselves:

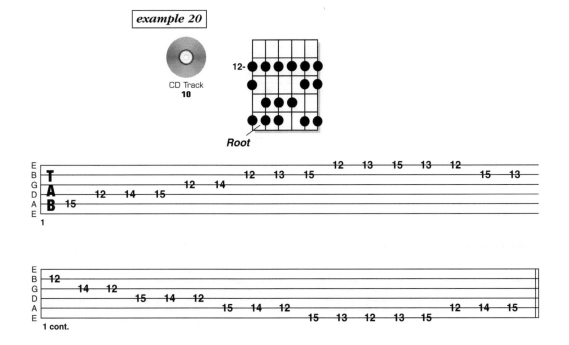

There it is; five shapes which cover the guitar fretboard with the notes from the scale of C major. Just to prove that there are only five and that the next one you meet if you continue upwards is the same as the first...

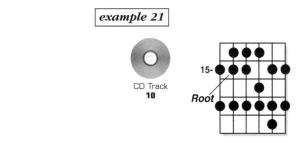

example 21

CD Track
10

Root

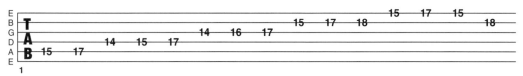

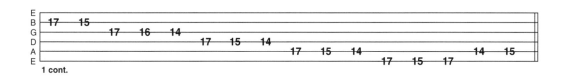

Point proved? I think so.

The next job is, just like with the Pentatonics, to start moving the major scale shapes around the neck before we get too familiar with a single key. We'll look at G next; here's the first shape you meet in the key of G major:

example 22

CD Track
11

Root

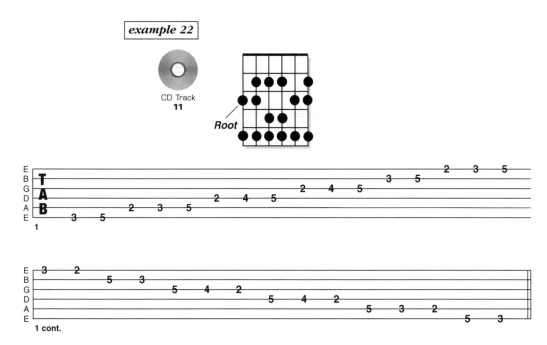

Recognise it? It's the same shape we met in C major at the eighth fret, but this time we're playing it at the third. Once again, you will probably find that it feels a little unfamiliar because of the extra stretch involved, having moved it down five frets. Here's the next shape:

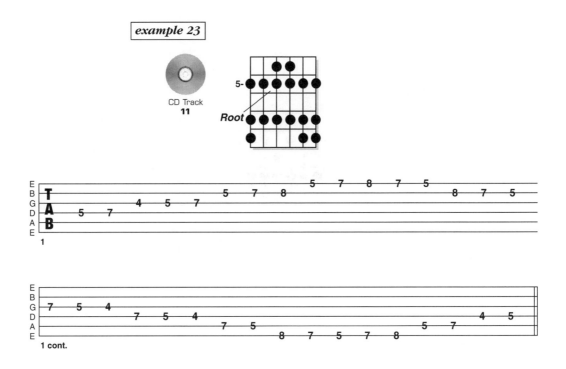

example 23

CD Track
11

After a while, you'll find that you can move from one shape to the next in any key without even thinking about it. For now, it's down to mental arithmetic and hard graft. Let's look at the third shape:

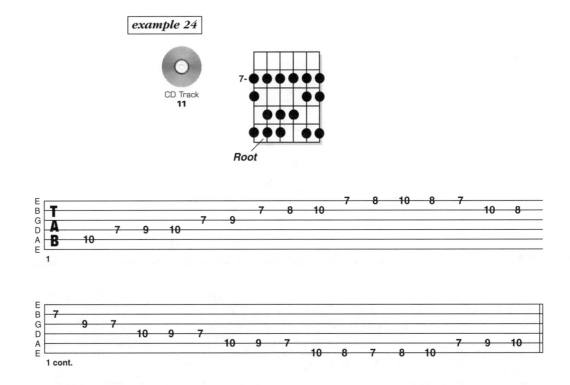

example 24

CD Track
11

The same but different. And the next:

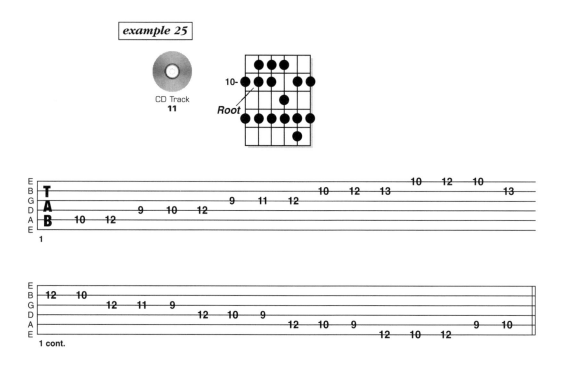

The last one completes the cycle for the second time...

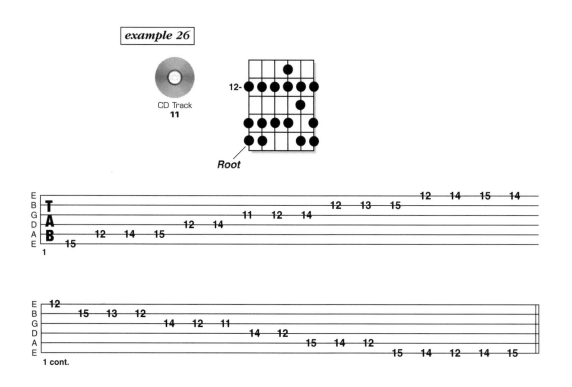

So now you've looked at the major scale in both the keys of C and G. Now, by referring to the neck chart you drew up for the barre chord chapter (you did do it, didn't you?) you should be able to find any major scale on the fretboard merely by matching up the root notes to the diagrams. Although it may seem confusing to begin with, remember that it's only a five-piece jigsaw and when you've been round the block with it a few times, you won't even have to think about it any more.

Be assured, you've covered a lot of very important ground in learning just these two scales.

The minor scale

I'll refer once again to the fact that no less than three minor scales exist in music, just in case you missed it the first time. Apart from the one we're going to look at, there is one called the 'melodic minor' and another called the 'harmonic minor'. I'll append both these scales to the 'miscellaneous' section at the end of this chapter just so that you can hear what they sound like, but we're not going to worry about them now.

So why have I chosen this particular minor scale, what does it do and what does it sound like?

To begin with, it's called the 'natural minor' (for reasons we'll talk about in a minute), but it's also known as the Aeolian Mode or Aeolian Minor, too.

As you progress with your studies you'll find that music is rife with its own synonyms. You get the impression that somewhere along the line someone was determined to make plumbing the depths of music's secrets as difficult as possible! No matter, we're going to call it the natural minor and have done with it – but don't be surprised if you come across the other names from time to time.

There's some very good news attached to the natural minor scale in the light of the work we've already done with the major equivalent; all the shapes for the minor scale are going to look extremely familiar to you. As an example, let's look at a shape for A minor:

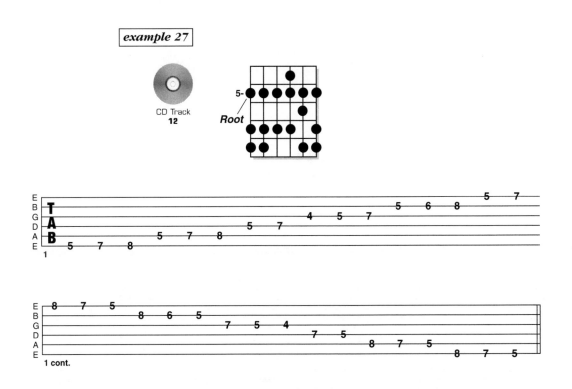

example 27

CD Track
12

Now, just to refer back to the major scales for a moment, check this shape out for C major:

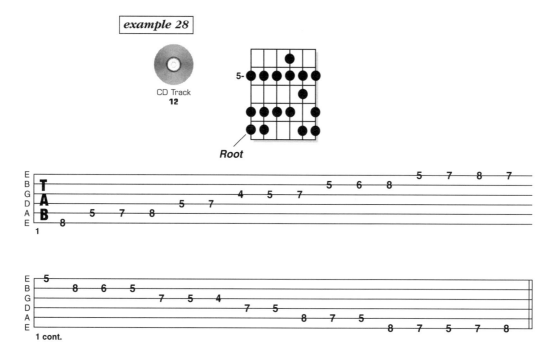

It's the same! It's just that the A minor version has its root notes in a different place – the fifth fret as opposed to the eighth. Apart from that, everything is pretty much as we left it a page or two back. Now I bet that's cheered you up a little...

The fact is that all the remaining shapes for A minor are the same as the ones we looked at for C major, too. So your fingers already know them. The important thing, then, is to play them from the new roots so that your ear gets to learn the sound of the new scale – your fingers have got a distinct advantage here, but don't rush or pass over A minor just because it feels like an old friend, it's vitally important that you learn the *sound* of the minor scale.

So here are the remaining four shapes for A minor:

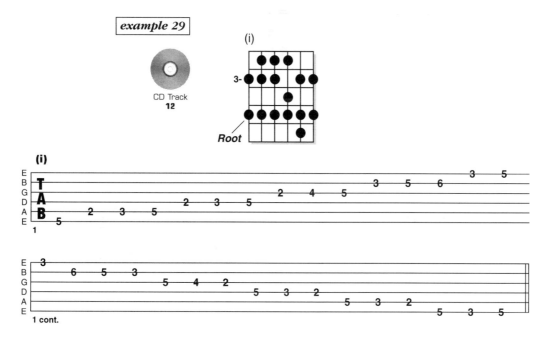

*example 29
continued*

CD Track
12

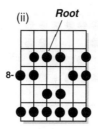

(ii)   *Root*

(ii)

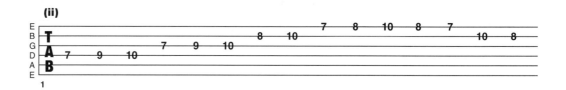

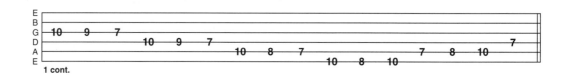

(iii)

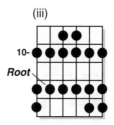

10-   *Root*

(iii)

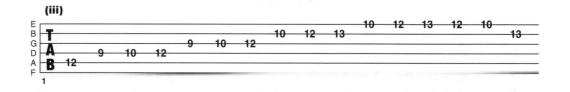

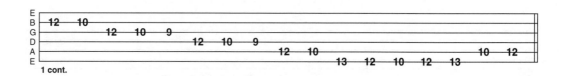

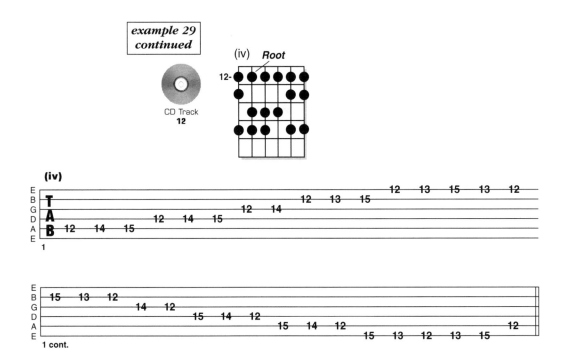

example 29 continued

CD Track **12**

(iv) **Root**

12-

(iv)

```
E |-------------------------------------------------------|
B |-------------------------------------12--13--15--13--12-|
G |---------------------------12--13--15------------------|
D |------------------12--14---------------------------|
A |--------12--14--15---------------------------------|
E |--12--14--15---------------------------------------|
   1
```

```
E |--15--13--12---------------------------------------|
B |--15--13--12---------------------------------------|
G |----------14--12-----------------------------------|
D |----------------15--14--12-------------------------|
A |------------------------15--14--12---------------12|
E |----------------------------------15--13--12--13--15----|
   1 cont.
```

In order that the minor scale system's movability becomes crystal clear, we'll look at the scale in another key, like we did with the major. I've chosen E minor for two reasons: one, because it's in all the same familiar places as G major, which we've already looked at and secondly, E minor is a very common rock guitar key. I do like the idea of getting optimum mileage out of all this stuff – but then, that's what this book is all about!

Here's the first shape:

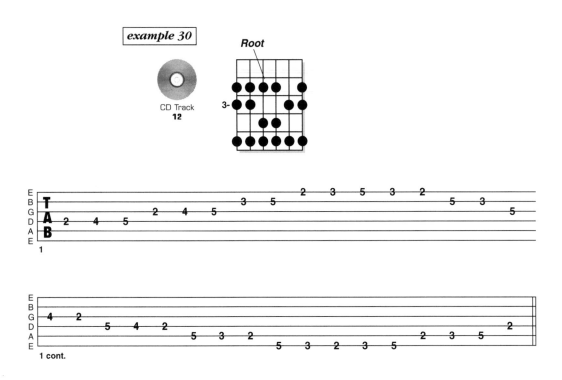

example 30

CD Track **12**

Root

3-

```
E |-------------------------------2--3--5--3--2---------------|
B |---------------------3--5-------------------5--3-----------|
G |---------------2--4--5-----------------------------5-------|
D |--2--4--5-------------------------------------------------|
A |---------------------------------------------------------|
E |---------------------------------------------------------|
   1
```

```
E |---------------------------------------------------------|
B |---------------------------------------------------------|
G |--4--2----------------------------------------2-----------|
D |--------5--4--2------------------------------------------|
A |--------------5--3--2---------------2--3--5--------------|
E |--------------------5--3--2--3--5------------------------|
   1 cont.
```

Needless to say, it looks the same as the G major equivalent, but the root notes are, once again, in different places. Here are its companions:

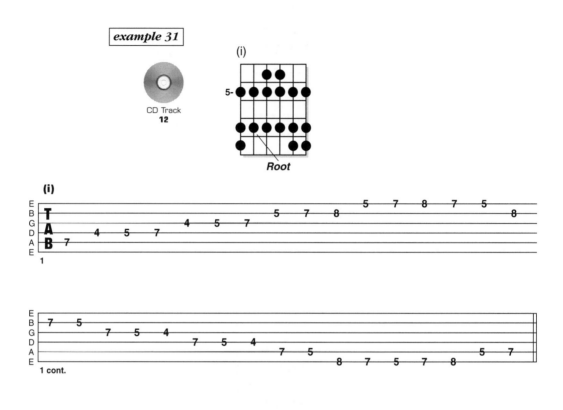

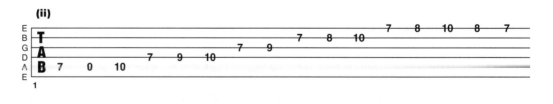

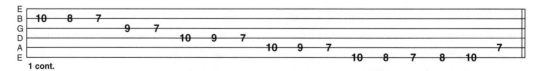

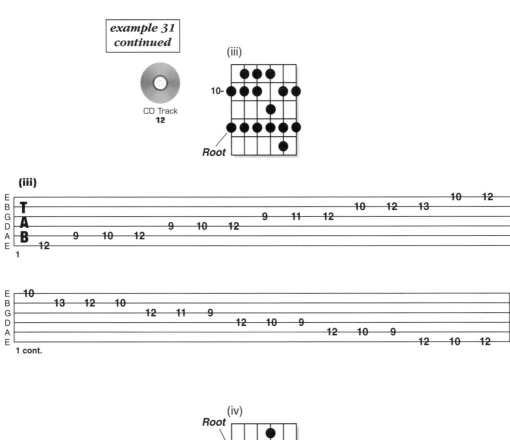

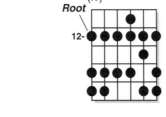

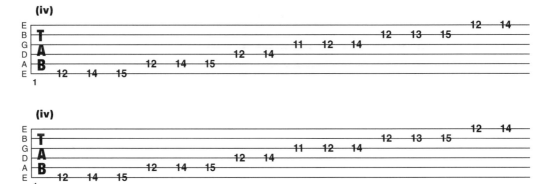

That really is the gist of the scale system for guitar; it's all done by shapes. Ask a pianist to play in D♭ and watch the blood drain from his face whilst he studies the keyboard and feels his self-respect seeping away.

Ask a guitarist the same thing and, if he's smart, he will just smugly move everything up one fret from C and carry on like he's got a PhD in playing in difficult keys. Nobody tell the keyboard player, OK?

The major Pentatonic

Believe it or not, I'm going to pull the same trick here, too. All the shapes we looked at when considering the minor Pentatonic are valid for the major version of the scale, it's just that all the root notes are in different places.

In case you needed the proof, here's one of the first shapes we looked at – this time, in the guise of C major Pentatonic:

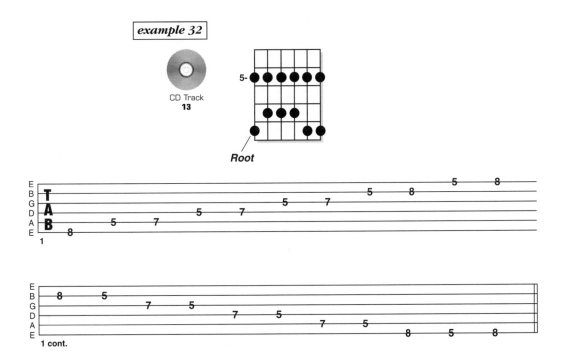

example 32

CD Track
13

Root

Play it through, but be sure to play it from root to root so that your ear gets to hear the difference between major and minor. Simple, huh? Now for the other shapes in the same key:

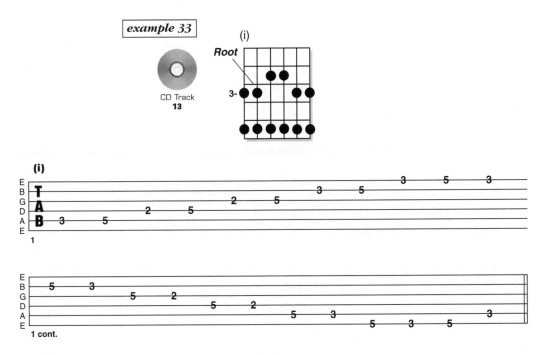

example 33

(i)

Root

CD Track
13

3-

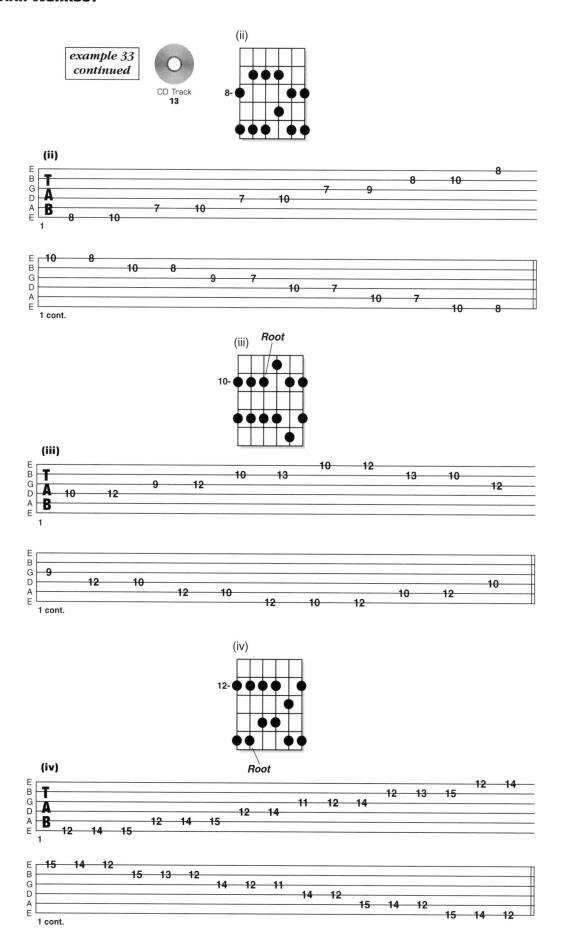

Watch out for those newly-positioned root notes. You'll soon get to know where they are by ear, but for now, we've got to take on a bit of work – fretboard orienteering, if you like.

Just so we remain consistent, we'll have a look at G major Pentatonic, too. Here's position one:

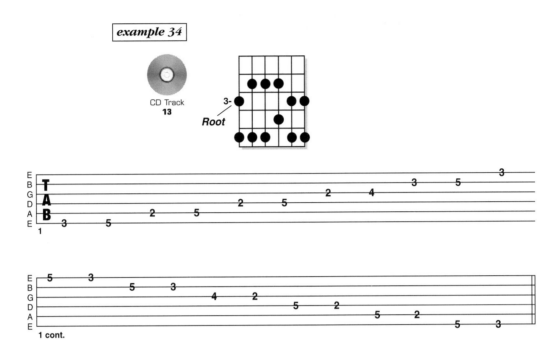

And, just for good measure, here's the rest:

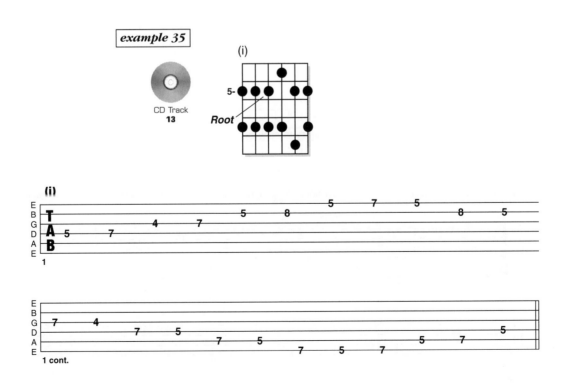

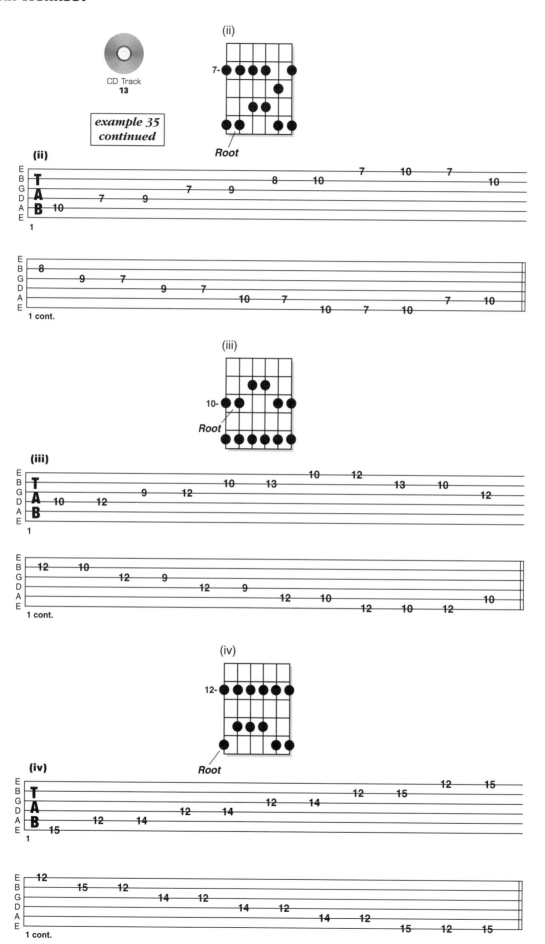

The difference in sound between major and minor scales is quite dramatic – even more so when you hear them in context. Some people tend to dismiss the both of the major scales we've looked at because they don't sound 'rock' enough. Worse still, there is a popular misconception that the major scales are only used in country music!

All four scale types we've looked at are of equal importance; you're exposing your ear to some vital information. If you choose never to take your guitar playing any further than just playing with friends or the occasional gig in a pub, you are harmonically very well-equipped. If you intend to pry further into music's exotica and learn some of the more colourful scales that exist, you have a very solid foundation on which to build. Virtually all scales are either major or minor in 'gender' and so this differentiation is of prime importance to imprint on the ear.

Let's take some time to listen to short examples of the scales we've looked at in context. First, here's the minor Pentatonic:

example 36
audio only

CD Track
14

Get the idea? Now, you might be thinking that this scale alone is enough for your soloing or melody playing needs, but listen to what you can do with the major scale:

example 37
audio only

CD Track
14

A lot of the time, people are amazed by what you can wring out of the major scale in a rock context. I mean, it sounds so innocuous when you play it on its own, doesn't it? Believe me, some of the greatest rock music (not forgetting jazz, pop, country, etc) has used that scale as a base. The minor scale is pretty useful, too...

example 38
audio only

CD Track
14

Remember that the minor scale can be viewed as being the minor Pentatonic with two extra notes and so it shouldn't come as much of a surprise that it fares so well in context. Those two notes make a big difference, don't they?

It's one of guitar's old wives' tales that you can't play rock or blues with the major Pentatonic. Wrong!

example 39
audio only

CD Track
14

When I've conducted guitar seminars in the past, it's always been one of my favourite questions to ask the assembled throng to name the guitar solos their ears just can't get a handle on at all. In general, most of the guitar players present have grasped the minor Pentatonic in a couple of positions and might have dallied a little with the natural minor, too. Just about 100% of the time the ear-dodging guitar parts have one thing in common – they're all drawn from the major scale.

This goes to show you how important it is to introduce your ear to both major and minor scales to ensure its musical education is well-rounded from the start.

If you detect that there might just be a single element missing from everything we've looked at already, you're right. We haven't looked at the blues scale.

Blues

When I was saying earlier that you only needed to learn four scales to get most places, musically speaking, I wasn't lying. We looked at four, saw there were only two sets of shapes between them and felt very pleased with ourselves as a result. Considering this, I feel that I'm still in credit if I tell you that we're going to look at the

blues scale. But before anyone reminds me that a deal's a deal – the most popular version of the blues scale is just a variation of the minor Pentatonic. In fact we're going to add a single note to it and witness an amazing difference. Here's the minor Pentatonic as you've already seen it:

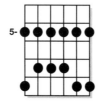

example 40

A MINOR PENTATONIC

And here's that extra note:

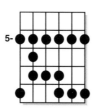

example 41

CD Track
15

A MINOR 'BLUES' PENTATONIC

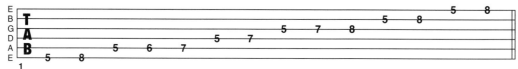

Naturally, it occurs twice in the diagram, but it's still only one note by name. This single note can be responsible for turning the minor Pentatonic into a very bluesy affair indeed. The note itself even has a special name – it's called the 'flat fifth'. That is, it's the fifth note of the minor scale, flattened (dropped one fret). You wouldn't think it made a whole lot of difference, but listen:

| example 42 audio only |

CD Track
15

Instant transportation to the Mississippi Delta! Of course, if we want to take things the whole distance, we've got to make sure to add all the necessary techniques like slides and so on (see chapter called 'What Special Techniques Do I Need To Know?'). In particular, we have to include bends – blues guitar is full of them – but we have to make sure we add them at a particular point. Here:

| example 43 |

CD Track
15

A MINOR WITH 'BLUES' 3rd

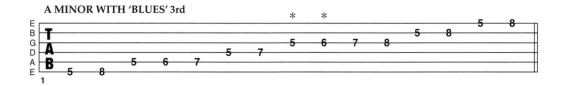

This note (the third) has a great significance in blues. We can't go into all the detail involved, but I will say that in blues, the pitch of this note is not precise. It varies between the two notes shown in the diagram and in order to be true to the genre, the only way we can get round the concept of there being an 'in-between' note sitting in the middle of the scale is to bend what we already have. Like this:

CD Track
15

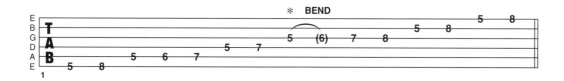

So, in context, you are going to hear the full blues scale sounding something like this:

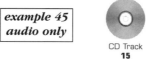

CD Track
15

It's sounding even blusier now, I think you'll agree. So, if we go through the other minor Pentatonic shapes once again, we'll see where the flat fifth and 'blue third' occur.

example 46

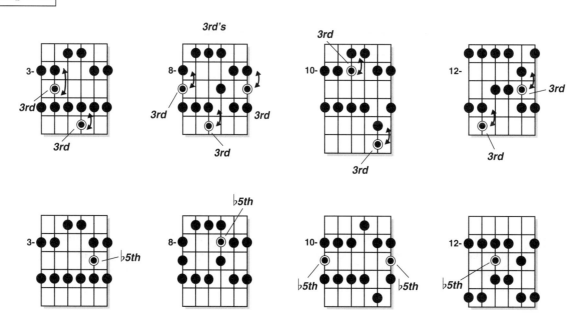

As you can see, from a fingering point of view, they don't always fall in the most convenient places – but guitarists have been coping with these shapes for years and playing some great blues music using them, nonetheless!

Surely that must be it?

Yes! If you were to learn the fingerings for all the above scales, got the knack of moving the shapes to all the keys and at the same time got your ears 'programmed' so that they recognised all of them, you could go practically anywhere (musically speaking) and not feel out of your depth.

You mean there are more of the critters?

Yes to that, too. It must be said that, in the main, any new scales you come across will be based on one of the ones you already know. For instance, they'll be either major- or minor-sounding and so you're already off to a head start. They might have exotic names and even more exotic applications, but there will always be some familiar ground that your ear will latch on to.

I'll give you a couple of examples of what I mean. You know I said that there are other minor scales? Well, here they are; first, the melodic minor:

example 47

THE MELODIC MINOR IN A

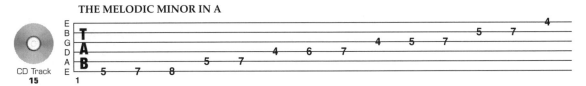

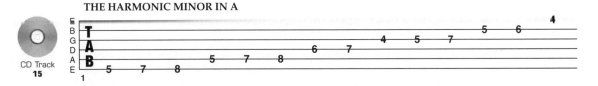

Now the harmonic minor:

example 48

THE HARMONIC MINOR IN A

The most important thing here is to recognise them as belonging to the minor scale family – and your ear will, given time and a decent practice schedule which guarantees to stretch and expand you.

Which order?

As to the exact order in which you should learn scales, learn all the 'non sharp or flat' keys first. This means, look at A, B, C, D, E, F and G before you start messing with any of the 'in between' notes. Playing a rock blues in the key of, say, B♭ is far less common than D or C. After a while, moving the scale shapes about is going to become second nature.

One last thing, remember that there are a few refined areas of music where you may need to put on your scalar bib and tucker, but it's not going to be very often and, if you learn these scales well enough, your ear will be ready to take on a little bit of musical exotica every so often.

what special techniques do I need to know?

The emphasis here is clearly set on the word 'need'. There are techniques you may want to learn a little further down the line – you might want to have a go at two hand tapping, playing slide, bending behind the nut and other assorted unlikely-sounding guitar tricks, but for now we'll concentrate on what you *need* to know.

Why 'need'? It can hardly be a life or death situation, after all, can it? There are a few techniques you've got to master before you'll be able to get certain run-of-mill sounds out of your guitar and the good news is that there are only really six, so relax.

Vibrato

The most important technique you have to master in the early days (well, months then) is called vibrato. It's a fundamental technique whereby physical movement is introduced to a note or chord after you've played it, just to give it a bit of a contour. Listen to the difference between these two notes:

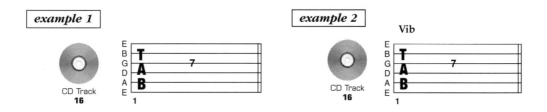

example 1 — CD Track 16

example 2 — Vib — CD Track 16

It's the same note, but doesn't the second example sound a bit more, ahem, rock?

Vibrato is, without a doubt, the most difficult technique you'll encounter in the early days of playing and that's why I start people off on it earlier rather than later. Resign yourself that it will take a while to get it sounding just right (it's a matter of muscle co-ordination and reflexes and that sort of thing takes time in the guitar gym!). But don't despair; I have never encountered a pupil who didn't master vibrato eventually. Just take some time out to practise it...

So how do you achieve perfect vibrato? It's all in the wrist, loosely speaking. The wrist and forearm act together in order to project movement into the fingertip and move the string fractionally from side to side. Let's look at it in degrees.

Stage one: let's play that note again, without any movement at all.

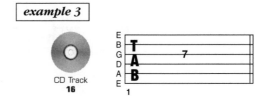

example 3 — CD Track 16

Play it with your third finger (it's probably the easiest finger to start with) and lay your first and second fingers behind it on the string – it will give some support. Now let's introduce some really slow, side to side movement. You are combining a slight 'push up and pull down' of the string into one, smooth movement. That's down towards the floor and up towards the ceiling, incidentally!

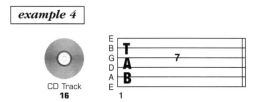

This is extreme slow motion, but essentially, all the elements are here. It may sound a little unlikely, but this is the beginning of the control you need to affect perfect vibrato and so don't try to run before you can walk and leave it at this level until you can get it to sound exactly like the CD.

The forearm/wrist movement should approximate that of turning a door handle with your left hand, but remember that all the movement generated has to be focused into your third finger. If it isn't, slow down even further and start again.

Once you've got a good-sounding slow vibrato, try speeding it up a little. The effect should now sound something like this:

CD Track
16

The movement in the hand, wrist and forearm is still the same, just a little faster. If it causes you trouble, remember that your finger is fighting against string tension of something like 16lbs and so vibrato is far from an easy technique to pull off.

Now, it's merely a matter of speeding up more and more, in stages, until you find that you're sounding something like this:

Once the fundamental side of vibrato is beginning to happen, try encouraging your other fingers to play our new game. Try adding vibrato with your first finger – did I tell you that it will probably hurt a bit? I didn't? Well, I expect you've found that out for yourself already anyway...

In any case, your first finger vibrato should sound very similar to the third finger – consistency is all, remember. Here's the sound of first finger vibrato:

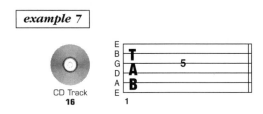

And now, in extremis:

example 8
audio only

CD Track
16

Didn't hurt a bit! If you need any more persuasion that vibrato is of deadly importance, I've devised another demonstration. Here is a brief snatch of a typical solo without vibrato:

example 9
audio only

CD Track
16

And here it is again positively popping with vib!

example 10
audio only

CD Track
16

Makes a difference, I think you'll agree. Once again, if you're having difficulty with vibrato, don't worry, it takes time, that's all. You will get it eventually and, what's more, it will become one of your musical instincts; you'll know exactly when, where and how to add it for best effect.

Vibrato on chords

It's possible to add vibrato to two or more notes at once. I feel another example coming on...

example 11

CD Track
16

```
E
B
G          5
D          5
A
E
  1
```

That was vibrato added to two notes played together. How about three?

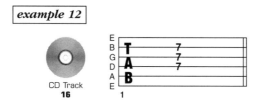

No problem. I should mention once again that nothing has significantly changed. The movement I'm using to add vibrato to multiples of notes is the same as if I was playing a single note; wrist and forearm with a slight 'door handle' turn to it.

Let's go for the full chord:

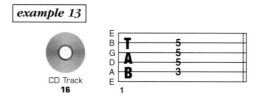

It certainly does something, doesn't it? Just in case you're not sitting there nodding, I'll play the same chord without any vibrato...

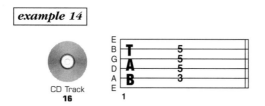

Vibrato is a technique which falls into the 'in constant use' category as far as guitarists are concerned. And it's not dictated by style, either; country, rock, jazz and blues players all use the technique – in slightly different ways, it's true. But scrape away the trappings of style and you've got the same basic technique consisting of muscle control and co-ordination. Simple as that!

Once you can control the technique – and this will come in time – you can add very subtle contours to your playing. Listen to the next example; the vibrato starts off slow and gradually speeds up slightly. Well, I like it...

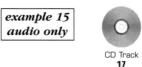

I should add at this point that the tremolo arm on your guitar (although 'tremolo arm' was precisely the wrong name to give the thing – it implies something entirely different) can achieve a very similar type of effect to finger vibrato. But trem arms are comparatively easy to get the hang of and so forgive me if I don't offer any directives here!

Bending

We're going to leave vibrato here for a while and look at the next important party trick in your guitar armoury – string bending. If you're intending to spend the rest of your life playing either classical or jazz guitar, I'll let you skip this section. They are about the only two areas of guitar playing where string bending isn't a fundamental necessity. And it's another hard one to master – I thought I'd be perfectly honest with you on this one...

So what does string bending actually achieve for the guitarist? Well, really all you're doing is travelling from one pitch (or note) to a higher one by pulling or pushing the string to a certain degree. You've all heard a guitarist bend a string at some time or other, but just in case you're still slightly confused as to what a bend sounds like, here's one I made earlier:

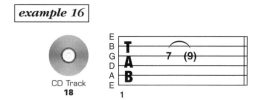

Technically speaking, all I'm doing here is travelling the distance between these two notes in one continuous movement:

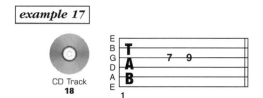

But the effect created by doing so on a single string has a certain finesse, n'est-ce pas?

So how do you go about learning to bend a string – and make it sound good and tuneful and not like a cat with its head caught in a mangle? You probably won't be at all surprised to know that, once again, it's down to muscle control and co-ordination and as such, it's unlikely that you'll be able to do it first time. These things need to be developed, remember.

First of all, we're going to try bending between these two notes:

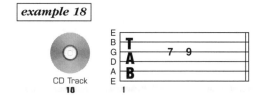

Play them to yourself as I've notated them above – like any journey, it's good to know your points of departure and arrival! Play both notes a few times and try to memorise them – it's your brain that's going to be in charge of things like pressure and it's going to have to know when to stop pushing (or pulling) the string. That is to say, when you've arrived at your 'pitch destination'.

Now, we're going to try our first bend with the third finger. Why? Well, it's pretty long and pretty strong, too, which makes it a good candidate for bender-in-chief. Oh and another thing, you probably use the third finger to bend more than any other... perhaps I should have mentioned that earlier.

When using your third finger to bend a string, it's very good practice to lay the first and second fingers down on the string behind the third finger

– just like you did when we were messing about with vibrato earlier. This will help guide your third finger while adding strength at the same time. Seeing as we're dealing with the third string, we're going to push the string 'up' (ie towards the ceiling). Incidentally, I chose the seventh fret for our first bend because the string is fairly 'loose' around here. Try this exercise at the third fret and you'll see just how much more of a fingertip shredder it could have been!

Your thumb should act as a sort of anchor point – something to pull or push against. Don't keep it behind the neck, most electric players make the most of thin necks and hook the thumb over the upper side of the guitar neck for good 'anchorage'.

As with just about every exercise in this book, start off slowly – nobody is standing over you with a stopwatch. A great many 'early learners' on the guitar get themselves into trouble by rushing things – and it only leads to heartbreak and half-cocked technique, believe me, so why bother?

Here's a demo of what you should be hearing:

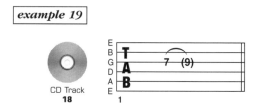

example 19

Good and slow, but most importantly accurate and on the button. I should probably point out at this point that most people experience a little discomfort the first few times they try to bend a string. Actually, that's putting it lightly; I've known pupils look at me silently pleading, 'Are you serious?' OK, so it's going to feel pretty strange at first, but those of you who drive will probably remember what it felt like the first time behind a steering wheel – you never thought you'd crack it, did you?

Another important thing to mention here is that this is all I want you to focus on for now; don't try bending other strings because you get bored with hearing good old D to E. Stick at it and measure your progress. After a little while, it will start to feel more and more natural and the 'push' isn't going to feel like riding white water in a kayak any more. It's going to be Sunday afternoon on the municipal boating pool before you know it!

Once you think that you've got your D to E bend pretty much hanging in there, we'll try another selection:

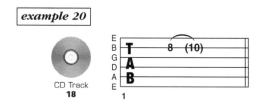

example 20

This is bending up from G to A on your second string. It shouldn't feel too different from our last little manoeuvre, and the rules are certainly the same; take your time, play the two notes individually every time you try it (in case you need to find them on the fretboard, here they are in tab):

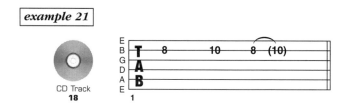

example 21

Focus in on the sounds of the two notes as you attempt to bend the string. If you've done your mental arithmetic correctly, you should be able to avoid 'under-bends' (aka bending flat) and 'over bends' (aka bending sharp). Your ear is going to tell you where to stop – and if you don't think it's too accurate for now, don't worry; it's going to get better – stick with it.

Once you can bend from one note to the next using the third finger in these two positions, make life difficult for yourself again by moving around the neck bending the G and B strings as before. You might end up with an exercise sounding something like this:

example 22

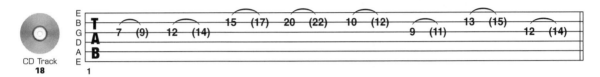

You'll find that the actual amount of bend is slightly different, depending where you are on the guitar neck. Don't despair; rely once again on your ears to tell you when to stop.

When it comes to the guitar's extremities, we have to alter our bending regime very slightly. Obviously, you can't bend the bass E string 'up' - you'd end up in mid-space above the fretboard. So you have to know how to 'pull' a string down to

bend it, too. In order to practise this, we can go back to our first bending exercise; seventh fret, G string, bending from the note D to E. Once again, play both notes separately first and then try 'pulling' the string down to the desired pitch. It's going to feel very odd the first time, but now you're more aware of the mechanics of the situation than you were before and so it shouldn't take too long to get the bend in the right general area. Here's a 'pull' type bend as an illustration:

example 23

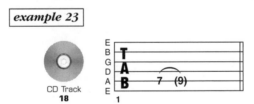

It sounds virtually the same as it does when you 'push' the string – and so it should. Bending strings is really one technique and should sound almost identical no matter whether you're pushing or

pulling.

As before, once your 'pulling' technique is as refined as your 'pushing' is, try moving around the neck, doing something like this:

example 24

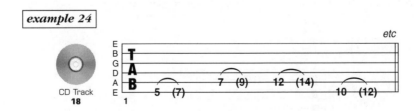

I'll repeat myself here and say that string bending is hard. It's hard on the fingertips and it's certainly not easy to achieve the right degree of accuracy straight away, but this is going to happen in time and it's only by repeating the few simple exercises above that we're going to achieve anything at all.

Is that it? Nope. The bad news is that you've got to be able to bend strings with every finger with the same amount of finesse as you're about to achieve with your third finger. The next victim on your left hand is your first, or index, finger... The index finger is called upon to bend strings quite frequently – just as it is called upon to add vibrato. But, because the technique is more difficult to perfect with your first finger, we're going to go easy on it and only ask it to bend a string half the distance the third finger had to travel. Listen to this:

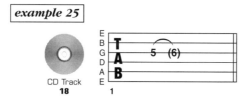

We're bending from the G string, fifth fret (the note C) to the sound produced by fretting at the sixth fret on the same string. Once again, here are the two notes in question:

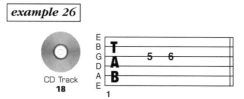

Play them one after the other until you can hum them to yourself. Now try bending with your first finger from one pitch to the next. Ouch, right? Well, I did say it was probably going to hurt at first...

Don't worry, eventually, you will develop hard skin on your fingertips and you'll hardly feel a thing!

Once you think that you've got the C to C# bend pretty much sorted out, try this:

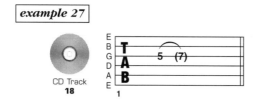

This time, we're going for the big one and bending a whole tone – C to D (fret 5 to fret 7). This can seem impossible the first time you try it, but it's no good seeking advice from the European Court Of Human Rights – ya gotta do it!

The good news at this point is that you're not expected to bend much further than this with your first finger and so, to all intents and purposes, this is as bad as it gets.

When your bending confidence really grows, you can start combining a bend with vibrato. In blues or rock styles of guitar, nothing sounds better than a good, emotional, controlled bend with added vibrato. Listen to this:

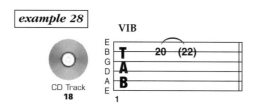

It's quite rock'n'roll isn't it? The two techniques are pretty much always combined into one on the shop floor – listen to this:

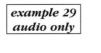

example 29
audio only

CD Track
19

Slides

Once again, we're going to leave vibrato and bending for a while to discuss another way guitarists have of travelling from one pitch to the other – known as 'sliding'. I'll say straight away that sliding isn't half as difficult as the first two techniques we've looked at so far in this chapter and so relax and take a little holiday – this is going to be a breeze!

With slides, you really know where you are – all you have to do is puzzle out where exactly it is that you're going and you're home free! Logically speaking, there are only two types of slide, too – up or down – and so that should make things even simpler. The main question is, how far are you going to go?

A slide is usually confined to either one or two frets and so the distance travelled is not too great. Listen to what a slide actually sounds like. Here's a slide upwards:

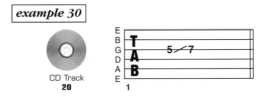

example 30

CD Track
20

And here's a slide downwards:

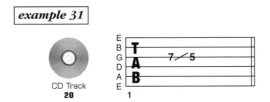

example 31

CD Track
20

Nothing to it, eh? But what on earth do we use a slide for? Here's a slide in context:

example 32

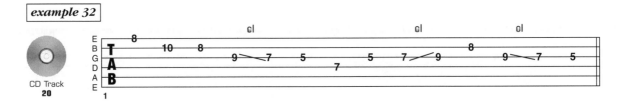

CD Track
20

Sound familiar? Good, I thought it probably would.

So what's actually going on here? I suppose there is a possibility that sliding actually sounds simpler than it is and so forgive me if I go into detail. Basically, all that's happening is that you're plucking a note and instead of holding it, bending it or adding vibrato, you're going to keep the flesh of your finger in contact with the string and the fretboard and move it along the string. And the first time you do it, it will probably hurt – who said this was going to be a breeze? I usually find that pupils fall into two categories if they can't quite get the knack of sliding: they either try applying too much or too little pressure, which affects the overall smoothness of the technique

somewhat. Another problem is that quite often, you need your brakes adjusted... Like anything in life, you need to know exactly when to stop and that's why we've got a little exercise to help us along the way. Here it is:

example 33

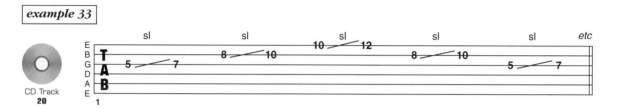

CD Track
20

You're moving the distance of two frets inclusively and using your first finger to do so. Try it.

The next thing to do is to move in the opposite direction:

example 34

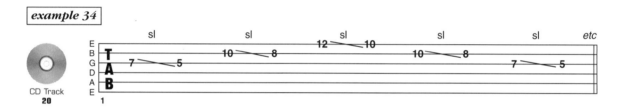

CD Track
20

Exactly the same as before, but now we're moving towards the left instead of the right.

Once you feel confident with this particular technique, add a smattering of vibrato (for now,

add a bit of vibrato to everything to see how it sounds – sometimes it sounds great, sometimes it doesn't). You should now have something resembling this:

example 35

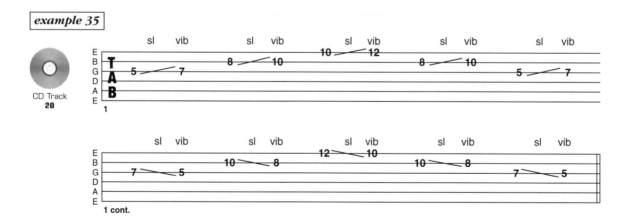

CD Track
20

Once you've got this pretty much sorted, just like we've done in the past, devise exercises that will challenge your new-found technical capacity. Try

playing along a single string, sliding to various points along it, something like this:

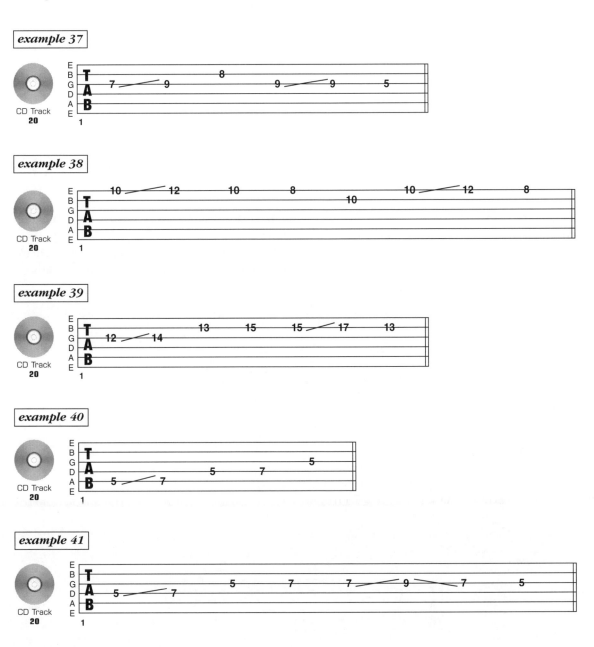

example 36

CD Track **20**

The enormous benefit from isolating a technique like this and practising it 'out of context' is that you're concentrating more on the correct execution of a single musical device, rather than having to think about merely adding it to a piece you're practising. It's all about focus.

From here on in, as far as sliding is concerned, you can take it as far as you want. Here's a couple of licks with slides in, just to give you an idea of how effective a technique it can be...

example 37

CD Track **20**

example 38

CD Track **20**

example 39

CD Track **20**

example 40

CD Track **20**

example 41

CD Track **20**

OK. So what's next?

Hammer-ons

Now here's another thing which is so fundamental to a guitarist's technique that half of them probably don't even realise they're doing it any more! A basic hammer-on is really just the art of sounding two notes from a single pick stroke. After the string is struck, another finger from the 'fretting' (ie left) hand 'hammers' down onto it, sounding a new note. Let's hear one:

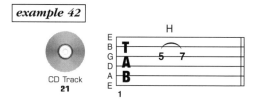

Here, I played the note at the fifth fret on the G string and 'flicked' my left hand third finger onto the seventh fret immediately afterwards. Let's compare the difference in sound if I had plucked both notes with the pick:

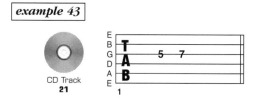

Sounds different, doesn't it? If we're going to make an exercise out of hammering-on, it would be to make sure that the volume between the two notes remains consistent; we don't want the 'hammered' note to sound quieter than the plucked note. So keep this in mind while you carry out the exercises.

Here's a selection of hammers to try – check with the CD to see if you can get them sounding dead right.

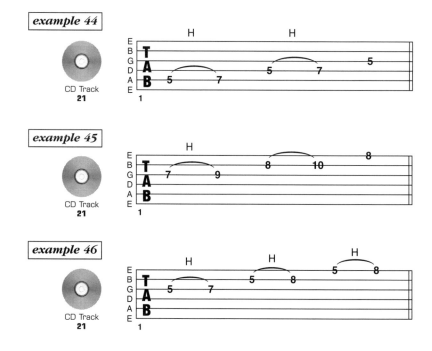

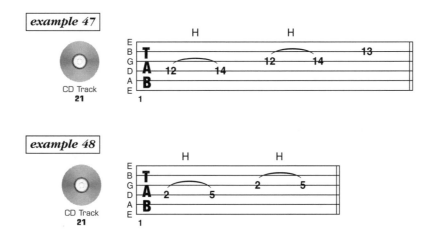

But how do hammer-ons (or 'hammers' for short) crop up in everyday playing? Let's look at this phrase:

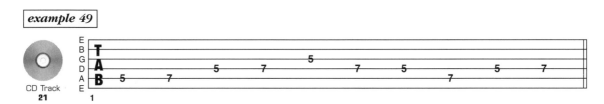

It's a regular bluesy phrase that could crop up in any one of a dozen musical situations (and sometimes it turns up a dozen times a night in the same musical situation!). But listen to how the edges have been rounded off a bit by employing a few hammers:

Now I think that sounds a whole lot better. The successful use of hammers can really make a phrase sing (and save some energy in your picking hand!). Here's a couple more:

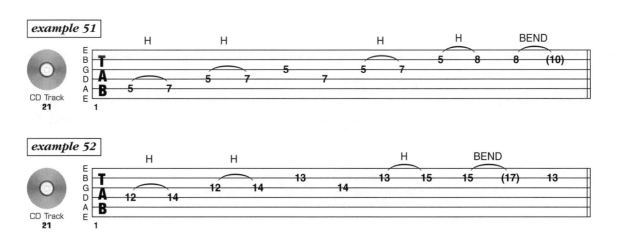

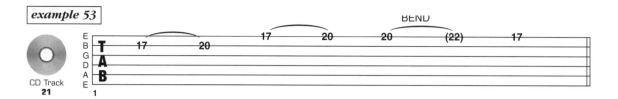

example 53

CD Track
21

It's probably the right time to mention a few words about cheating. People will tell you that hammering is 100% easier if you turn the gain up on your amplifier (if you have one). Well, I'm not denying it; whacking the gain up on your amp can make a lot of things feel easier – your whole 'pluck to note volume' ratio moves into another dimension... But!

I would really suggest that you master the art of hammering without the guitar plugged in... seriously. The point is, if you get this technique right without any artificial additives like monster gain, you can make all sort of stylistic adjustments later on. For now, you have to go cold turkey and get the basics right...

Pull-offs

It was Newton who announced to the world that every action had an equal and opposite reaction and that's certainly true of hammer-ons. Their

equal and opposite reaction is called the *pull-off* and it sounds like this:

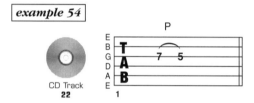

example 54

CD Track
22

It's tempting to think that all you have to do to pull off the perfect pull-off is reverse the process, pluck the higher note, remove the finger from the fret and bingo! - the lower one will sound. Nope. Sorry, it's not quite that easy. Consider this scenario: you're using the same fingers as before; first finger on the fifth fret G string, third finger

on the seventh fret G string. If you want to effect a good pull-off, you have to pluck the string with your left hand third finger as you remove it. Nothing too much, just a slight sideways movement will do the trick. If I exaggerate the movement, you can actually hear what's going on a whole lot clearer:

example 55 audio only

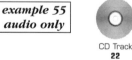

CD Track
22

If it sounded like I cheated and struck the second note with a pick, I didn't; what you heard was just flesh being dragged across the string.

This is only for demonstration purposes, of course. In a real playing (or even practising) situation, you'd strive for the same thing as before; two notes of equal volume like this:

example 56 audio only

CD Track
22

So, once again, if we take a musical phrase played without pull-offs (aka 'pulls') it would sound like this:

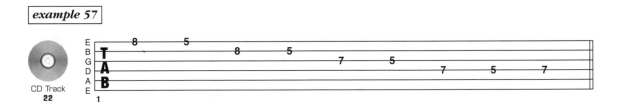

But once we add a few pulls, we achieve the same sort of effect as before – everything 'smooths out' somehow.

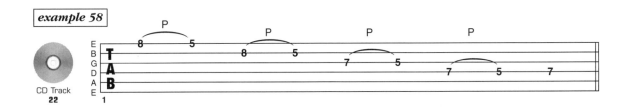

And if you combine the two – hammers and pulls – you can achieve things like this:

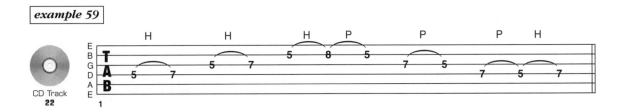

Don't worry too much about the musicality or the context of these playing examples to start with. If you remember my comparison between the guitar and a typewriter for a moment, these techniques all come under the heading of 'physical development'. We'll address your musical development later on!

A good exercise to help you combine these two effects would sound something like this:

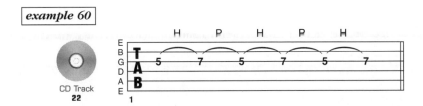

Now here it's important that you follow some good advice and practise the last example very slowly to start with. You're probably coming to this technique with 'soft' muscles and I don't want you to hurt yourself. It's the kind of thing that could very easily put the hand into cramp – and that hurts, so be careful. Take things easy and stop at the first sign of discomfort. As you gain more and more control, speed things up gradually. Which kind of brings us onto the next technique...

Trills

If you've followed everything through so far, you'll find that you can already half do a trill. It's a combination of hammer and pull and it sounds like this:

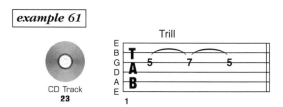

Once again, we're in position with the first finger positioned on the fifth fret, G string and the third finger dead set on playing the seventh fret on the same string. First, you hammer from the fifth to seventh, but instead of leaving your third finger in place, you instantly perform a pull, ending up where you started.

Usually, a trill will be followed by another note like this:

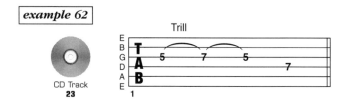

Furthermore, you will more often than not hear it in context like this:

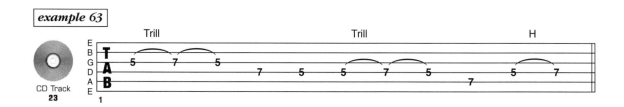

Of course, you'll get trills, hammers and pulls over two frets, three or even four and so a decent exercise could sound something like this:

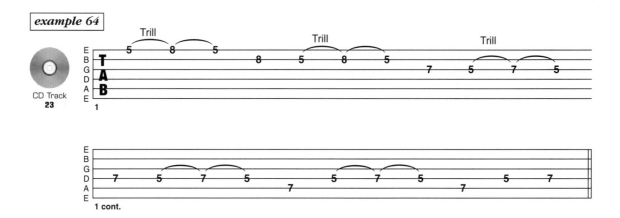

What's more, all the above techniques are likely to happen pretty much continuously during a guitar solo or melody part – independent of style or anything, they're all common to most of the 'popular' styles of playing.

So if you add vibrato, bending, slides, hammers, pulls and trills together, things are going to start sounding like this:

CD Track
24

Pretty standard blues/rock fare, wouldn't you say? The point is that by isolating all of these techniques and spending a little time improving each of them, it gives you a chance to develop them quicker.

Don't worry if the last example is well out of reach technically – it was only meant as a demonstration of how the effects sound 'in the field'. Once again, we'll worry about scales and so on a bit later.

Did I say six techniques?

If we were really going to split hairs, I guess you could say that there are seven (we could go on subdividing all night, too). One important technique which has an overall influence on your playing would be muting. I haven't included it as a separate technique in its own right, because you'd apply it to everything we've looked at so far.

Muting is a thing which most guitarists fall into naturally. If you strike the strings with the right hand and leave them ringing, the sound tends to take a few seconds to die away naturally. A lot will depend on which guitar you're playing at the time, acoustic or electric, loud amp or quiet, that sort of thing, but essentially there is always a little 'ring on'. Sometimes, this can actually add something to the music we're playing, other times, if for instance

you're playing quite a fast rhythm part, you'll find that your playing begins to lose a lot of its definition if you allow the strings to ring on for too long. This is where muting comes in. I would imagine that the way muting was 'invented' was merely by early players of the instrument placing their right hands on the strings to silence them and it gradually evolved from there.

In practice, a guitarist will be muting most of what he does; it's a way of 'editing' your playing and keeping the rhythmic content crisp and well-defined. The technique itself involves the fleshy part of the right hand (the 'edge' of the hand from little finger to wrist) resting gently on the strings just in front of the guitar's bridge. The difference is pretty much apparent from the onset; here's an unmuted chord:

example 66

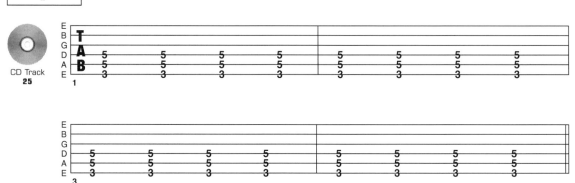

And here's one which I've tamed a bit with some muting:

example 67

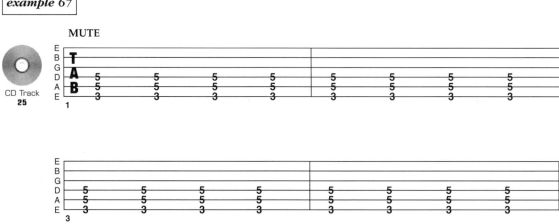

Can you hear the effect? The second example sounds a little bit more under control, somehow. The way I always introduce pupils to muting is let them explore the technique for themselves, having defined for them the parameters between which they will be working. Realistically, the two points we're working between are a totally unmuted chord (as in the example above) and a totally muted 'thunk' (which I'll leave to your imagination!). By working between these two 'bookends' you can find for yourself every point which lays between.

So what do we use it for? Well, just about everything! Here's a rhythm part which just wouldn't be the same in a totally 'hands off' situation...

example 68
audio only

CD Track
26

And here's a riff passage which also lives and breathes thanks to the intervention of the right hand.

**example 69
audio only**

CD Track
27

At first, you may find that muting is cramping your style a bit – literally, because the right hand's sense of uninhibited movement has been interfered with. After a while, you'll find that you're muting automatically without necessarily being conscious of what you're doing.

It's the type of technique, as are all the others we've looked at in this chapter, that you can add to your DIY workout later on as an area in your playing which needs isolating and developing. It's only by looking at a single technique and focusing in on it exclusively that you will give it a real chance to mature. The idea of letting nature take its course in this respect, is the long way around!

Left-hand muting

The left hand is responsible for some muting work, too; although arguably its work is more subtle. Left-hand muting can be as simple as merely lifting the fingers slightly having struck a chord so that you cut it dead. Like this:

example 70

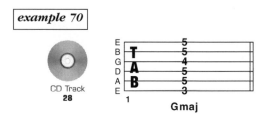

CD Track
28

Gmaj

All that's happening there is a slight release in grip in the left hand – don't take the hand away completely or lift the fingers clear of the strings because that way you'd be back in the 'unrestrained sustain' area.

The other method of muting with the left hand is to use any available finger or fingers (ie the fingers that aren't involved in playing at that particular time and are 'going spare') to gently touch the strings while playing. It has almost the same effect as right-hand muting, but the difference is a subtle one.

When the left hand is really given its rein and allowed to shape a chord passage via muting, it can achieve very positive results. But how do we decide which hand is in charge of this vital area at any one time? The easy answer here is that when the right hand is busily involved in a rhythm passage and is literally too busy or active to worry too much about muting, then the left hand takes over. But of course, there is more to it than just that! It's really a case of the sum of the parts working together to produce a satisfactory whole.

It's a darned difficult thing to teach, too! Which is why I usually merely tell pupils about it, offer a few examples of the effects that can be achieved using muting and let them experiment on their own.

As I've said above, all these techniques ought to be looked at in isolation and as part of a practice routine. Spend some time every day checking out how your bending and vibrato is getting on – if it's still not quite right, don't panic, just keep working on it and it will slowly develop. The trick is not to ignore any of the above and just leave things to chance, hoping everything will sort itself out. It won't. I've known guitarists who have been playing for years who tell me that a couple of things about their playing still don't quite go the distance – but they generally follow it up with 'I guess I should have practised it a bit when I started out...' And if there was ever an author's message, that was it!

what's all this about ear training?

I once saw a diagram in a book which set out to explain how ear training helped the modern 'rock' musician (yes, it was one of those books that put quote marks around words like 'rock'. You know the sort, I'm sure). The diagram showed a gramophone (I'm serious), an ear, a brain and a pair of hands. They were all linked together in that order and the idea was that the ears heard something, the brain translated that into 'guitar data' and the hands played it. Now believe it or not, that book had got it about right...

Traditionally, rock musicians differ from their classical counterparts in at least one crucial department although both will have a keen sense of music. But a classical musician is, to a large extent, taught to play the notes he sees on the page, inject the necessary feeling and emotion into the music and voilà – his job is pretty much done. The rock musician will tend to memorise all the music he performs and will probably never play it exactly the same way twice, either. He will also improvise to a certain extent; that is, he will use musical ideas he has in his head which correspond to the key and nature of the piece he is playing. He will probably also be required to play a completely alternate melody line at some point, off the top of his head. Enter the improvised guitar solo!

So obviously players involved in 'non-formal' music (you see, I can use quotes, too!), that is to say music which isn't necessarily pre-composed or written down, have to rely on their ears a fair deal.

Now not everyone is born with a great musical ear. It's a thing which 99% of the time has to be learned and developed the same as everything else. There are just different starting-off points... You've probably heard people refer to either themselves or others as being 'tone deaf'. Well I have personally never met anyone who was both tone deaf and interested in music; I've heard about a couple of people who seem to have some sort of 'block' in terms of the link between enjoying music internally and being able to express it via either voice or instrument, but I've never actually met one. I believe that most of the time a totally non-musical ear belongs to someone who has a total non-interest in music (and I've met plenty of them!).

At the other end of the scale, you've maybe heard of people who are said to have 'perfect pitch'. That is, the ability to recognise a note and name its pitch just like you or I would be able to name a colour. Now I have met a few people with perfect pitch and all claim that it was always there – they didn't develop it, it was always something they were aware of from their very first encounters with music. One told me that it wasn't necessarily an asset to him as a musician, either. Although I must say, speaking as someone who has fairly good but nowhere near perfect pitch, I can't really see too many disadvantages.

The truth is, most people fall somewhere in the middle of these two extremes; their active interest in music, perhaps expressed through learning an instrument, puts them in a situation where what they have in terms of a musical ear, is forced to develop. But my experience has shown me that if ear training is included as part of your practice schedule, good results will be achieved much faster than if it's all just left to chance.

If you think about the diagram I mentioned at the beginning of this chapter, you'll see that connecting what the ear hears to what the fingers play is an essential part of becoming a musician. As an example, I bet there are people out there who have said at one time or another that they wish they could play the things which they hear in their heads. Well, ear training is the way of bringing that about. We've just got to get those ears transmitting all the right information to the hands and on to the fretboard.

One of the most simple ways of bringing this trick about is to sing everything you play. It's a bit like the difference between reading a book out loud or reading to yourself; reading out loud makes you focus far more on every word, whereas reading to yourself means that you tend to 'scan' whole sentences rather than actually reading them.

Now I'm aware that the process of gaining some sort of 'pitch awareness' can be a bit of a slog. But it's far from an impossible task. To start with, you could try playing any old note on the guitar and try to hum it. You might find that, to begin with, you're miles away from the right note, or that you are close but not spot on. As you work more with chords, scales and the other music-learning trench work that has to be done to begin with, you'll find that your ear picks up more and more on what you're doing. It might start out as a mechanical process to begin with, with your fingers merely obeying instructions from the page, but there is a time when the ear clicks in and from then on the link between brain and fretboard begins to become established.

I tell most of my pupils to sing the scales as they play them. This way, two things are happening at once; co-ordination and muscular development on one hand, and the ear is beginning to associate what the fingers are doing with what it's hearing on the other. In other words, the brain is sitting in the middle controlling muscles, but also being fed other vitally important musical information at the same time. Things start to link up pretty quickly,

believe me.

Another way of getting the ear to 'tune in' was recommended to me ages ago and I found it very helpful indeed. Buy yourself a tuning fork (they are a few pounds from music shops). They are available in different pitches, but go for an 'A 440' if you can. That's the pitch of the top E string at the fifth fret. Keep your tuning fork with you all the time and every so often, take it out, hit it against something, listen to the note it produces and try to hum it. You will find, because you're dealing with only a single pitch, that your ear tends to 'hone in' on the note eventually; you've given it a sort of easy landmark to remember. Repeat this action at various points during the day for a few weeks until you can almost hear the note before you tap the tuning fork. Then, try humming the note beforehand, checking afterwards to see if you were right. You'll find that you get close every so often – other days you might still be well away.

Later on, you'll find you can play games with the tuning fork by humming harmony notes, arpeggios, scales, intervals and so on, all from this one note. At this stage, your ear will really be developing quite nicely, but I appreciate that this level of ear training might well lie some time in the future for most people. I mention it primarily because it's a musical activity which will be of immense value to you, but you don't have to be anywhere near a guitar in order to do it.

Still the most important thing to do is to tie what your ear is hearing into what's happening on the fretboard and so humming scales is going to do for now. As discussed in the chapter which deals with scales, the first and most important job for the ear is to learn to differentiate between major and minor tonalities.

Ear training programme

You'll be including a little ear training in your daily practice routine and so, after the initial stages, you'll probably be referring back to this chapter fairly often for fresh ideas.

As I've already pointed out, music is built on scales and chords – harmony and melody. So making the ear aware of these staples is going to be of incredible long-term advantage to anyone who wishes to play a musical instrument at any level. Even if you want to sit in your living room and play only for your own amusement, this kind of training is going to make things easier and a lot more musical.

Having already picked notes at random and tried to sing them, and by singing the scales as you play them you will have built up a fairly solid foundation on which to build more and more musical awareness.

The next step is to play the scale on the guitar, but miss notes out, singing them instead of playing them. In other words, instead of playing this:

example 1

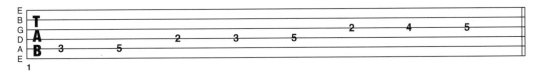

You'll be playing this, singing the notes marked with an asterisk:

example 2

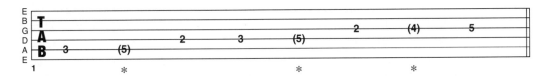

You can do the same with chords, too. Start by playing and singing something like this:

example 3

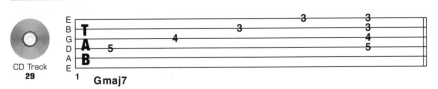

Then try singing the chord before you actually play it – just give yourself the first note and fill in the blanks. Then check yourself to see if you were right.

example 4

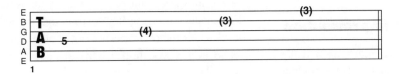

As you will see from the charts, you'll be expected to do a little of this kind of thing every day. How much further you take it is up to you. You'll have achieved a fair amount just by attaining 90% accuracy on the kind of thing I've suggested already.

Advanced ear training

The simple thing here is that ear training is always going to be more of the same; singing and playing, testing and teasing the ear to see if it can go everywhere the fingers can.

Once you are fairly sure-footed with the major and minor scales and major and minor chords, try playing only the root note of the scale and singing different notes from it, like this:

example 5

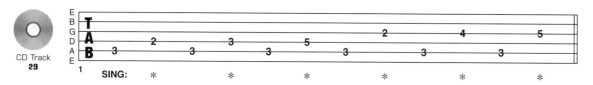

CD Track
29

Don't panic here! The note belongs to the scale, you're just unfamiliar with the leap from root to scale tone without the support of all the other notes which lead up to it. Just try to hear the notes in between in your head. If necessary, hum silently up to the note you want before humming it. Anything you can do to test and stretch your ear musically has got to be worthwhile. You're building a link between the eyes, ears and fingers and, although it might seem like a lot of work, the results are going to be worth the effort.

Later on, you could try playing the melody to some well-known tunes. I mean really well-known stuff like nursery rhymes, too. Don't try to work out anything that you can't hum all the way through beforehand. When you begin to reverse the whole ear training process I've outlined above and ask the brain to 'play back' rather than 'record' information, you've got to give it the best possible chance. Nursery rhymes benefit from being a) very simple and easy to remember and b) they've been programmed into you from birth and so they're fairly well ingrained into the psyche.

Make it a rule that the most you can expect from your ear is that if you can hum it, you should be able to play it. If you can't hum it, you don't know it and so you're expecting a bit much!

A word or two about improvisation

This sort of 'play what you hear' mechanism really comes into play during improvisation. The principle here is that when a musician plays anything, he's hearing it in his head first. It doesn't originate from the guitar fretboard, it begins in the brain. I can remember having great difficulty understanding this concept when I was a mere musical stripling. I couldn't see how it was possible to hear notes in my head before I played them. If this was the root of improvisation, how was it possible for me to learn to do it? I've since learned, of course, that we all improvise every day of our lives.

Try a simple experiment: imagine I've just asked you what your favourite holiday of all time was and why. You'd probably have no difficulty telling me the location, approximate dates, what you did, where you went – and maybe even who you met. In other words, I asked you a question and you improvised a reply. You weren't reading your answer from some prepared text, you were relying on your memory, your ability to communicate with me via a common language and many other things besides which you were totally unaware of – like syntax, grammar, colloquialism, parody, oxymoron etc. What's more, assuming that your story didn't come out in a jumbled, incoherent string of nonsense, you must have had some sort of idea what you were going to say before you said it. You were able to simultaneously organise and formulate your thoughts as you went along.

Musical improvisation is nothing more or less than the task you performed by telling me the sordid details (you wish!) of your Club 21 holiday to Majorca. I gave you a theme and a subject and you improvised with it. In music, your subject and theme is probably down to such things as key, rhythm, melody and more besides, but the two tasks are not at all dissimilar.

So even if you find it hard to believe that your musical thoughts will ever flow as freely, naturally and spontaneously as your recollections of some good times on holiday, hold on to the idea that you will soon develop enough musical grammar, syntax and so on to tell some tuneful stories of your own!

what are effects units?

It won't be long before you feel yourself wanting to buy yourself some more guitar-related gear, you can be sure. It's fairly addictive, all this guitar business! But I have been asked so many times in lessons what effect I think a student should buy – and it's an almost impossible question to answer. Everyone wants their first effects unit to be one that makes a big difference to the way they sound, but no one is ever sure exactly what all the various units sound like or how they affect the guitar's sound. Fair enough; it's an effects jungle out there and so excuse me while I whip on my pith helmet and volunteer to be your guide!

Let's start at a very basic level; an effects unit is an electronic gizmo which you place in between you and your amplifier to somehow modify your sound. They can cost anything from around £50 to £5000 and above for top-of-the-range studio units and they also vary in appearance to the same degree.

You may have heard guitar players refer to 'stomp boxes'; these are effects units which spend their life on the floor, the idea being that, when you need to switch them on, you merely 'stomp' on their cunningly reinforced switches and bingo – you're in. These are by far the most common type of units (and quite often the cheapest) and you will see many players with a whole series of them wired together like a daisy chain on stages all over the country. In the main, they are battery-powered (although some are so power-hungry, it's futile to consider anything other than a mains adaptor at time of purchase) and will usually boast an array of knobs so that you can adjust their sound-transforming wares to taste.

Another floor dweller is the multi-effects unit. These are larger than the ordinary stomp boxes and the modern variants tend to look like something you'd find on board the Space Shuttle. It's not uncommon to find LED readouts, flashing lights and other details which add even more to the overall military appearance. Oh, and they're usually black, too and, rumour has it, that they are invisible to enemy radar...

The final contender for effects design is the 'rack' unit. During the 80s, banks of stacked effects started appearing behind the world's guitar players, contained in specially built housings which looked a lot like upright domestic freezers. (Only they were covered in flashing lights and LED readouts.) The idea was to get all your effect needs neatly stored away and off the floor. What's more, the computer revolution meant that effect units could be pre-programmed so that you could have different set-ups for every song.

Almost simultaneous with this came MIDI and wireless systems. Once upon a time, it was only keyboard players who knew what MIDI stood for; it's a mnemonic and stands for Musical Instrument Digital Interface, which sounds very mysterious, but it's basically a digital language which one keyboard/effects unit uses to talk to another one. With the computer age well and truly upon us and schoolchildren ably surfing the Internet while we try to make sense of the office networking system, MIDI isn't quite the culture shock it once was. Guitarists are natural Luddites and renowned techno-phobes (think about it, we use 50s design guitars and valve amps, for heaven's sake!) and, although MIDI was initially welcomed – albeit cautiously – current trends tend towards a 'back to basics' ethic and once more, stomp boxes are being brought out of closets world-wide and returning once again to the rock'n'roll stage. Most stomp boxes shun digital technology and hence stand in line with our choice of guitars and amplifier.

I mentioned wireless systems and I'd better offer a pocket explanation here, too. Basically, a wireless system comprises a radio transmitter and receiver. You plug your guitar into the transmitter, plug the receiver into your amp and throw away your guitar lead. You're suddenly free to wander the stage at will without the constraints of a guitar lead. It has to be said that wireless systems really

come into their own on huge stages – we're talking stadiums here, not a 12'x15' area in the corner of a pub! Good wireless systems are expensive and the ones you see in the big concert venues have probably cost their owners thousands. I generally tend to advise people to leave this accessory until last on their shopping lists...

I must say here that effects units should only really be seen as the icing on the cake – they will only add to what's there already and will not make playing any easier!

So what are all the different effects called, what do you use them for and what do they sound like?

We'll take advantage of the CD here and I'll at least be able to illustrate the use and abuse of the more common effects to you.

Distortion devices

Here, the effect's name speaks pretty much for itself. Not all amps come with an inbuilt facility to produce distortion, gain or overdrive (which are all basically the same thing in the end) as part of their 'act'. Certainly amps built during the 60s would only distort if you turned them up to ear-abusing levels and so some sort of external

distortion-producing device is essential for a peaceful coexistence with family, friends and neighbours.

Distortion units do basically one thing – they distort your guitar signal. The way they do it, or certainly the end result, varies enormously. Here's our first example:

example 1 audio only

CD Track
30

If you haven't got an amplifier with a 'gain' or 'overdrive' control, a distortion pedal might very well be your point of entry into the world of effects. Certainly if you want to play anything remotely rocky

or bluesy. It's only really jazz and certain country styles which avoid distortion altogether. (I'm taking for granted that classical guitarists and acoustic guitarists might just be ignoring this chapter...)

Chorus

This is an effect which is almost impossible to describe either in print or by word of mouth. I'm not even going to try and explain how it works electronically, save to say that the guitar's signal is mixed back with itself in a slightly altered, delayed state, giving the sound a 'wash' or 'ambience'. Let's hear an example:

example 2
audio only

CD Track
30

Today, most chorus units are stereo which is great in the studio, but expensive to run live (ie you need two amplifiers). Chorus is great for rhythm work as it gives some sort of contour to your sound. Chorus can also be used to 'smooth out' distortion in a multi-effects situation, as we'll see later on.

Reverb

This is another effect which often comes in-built with amplifiers. Your guitar signal is delayed and fed back on itself to produce the effect of playing in a pre-defined, 'virtual' space. Short for 'reverberation', you can hear this effect by clapping your hands together in a cave or cathedral and listening to the sound slowly decay around your head.

Once, reverb was created by using a series of springs to electromechanically delay your guitar signal, but the 'digital age' saw the effect really come into its own. Now, it is possible to be very precise about the exact size of the artificial environment you wish to place your guitar sound within – all in glorious stereo, too!

Let's take a few examples:

example 3
audio only

CD Track
30

That was a 'small room' reverb. It's arguable that the precise control over reverb really has the most effect in a studio environment and you can probably imagine that the studio reverb units have an almost unfathomable degree of variation. We'll deal here with some of the extremes, just to give you some idea...

example 4
audio only

CD Track
30

That was a 'large hall' – and you'll probably agree that it would pass for the sound of a guitarist playing on his own in a venue like London's Royal Albert Hall. But if the RAH is still too modest a venue for you, how about a sports stadium?

| example 5 |
| audio only |

CD Track
30

Not bad, eh? Believe it or not, there are a few settings on many of the studio-based reverb units which exceed even a sports stadium. You want extra-large? Here's the reverb equivalent of outer space!

| example 6 |
| audio only |

CD Track
30

Echo

Another effect which is very similar to reverb is echo – also known as 'delay'. The first echo units contained a loop of recording tape and many playback heads which you could shift around mechanically to simulate varying delay times. Once again, the digital age saw the whole process computerised and made more accessible, accurate and affordable. Digital delay units are now commonplace in a guitarist's effects array and have a great deal to do with the sound you hear either live or on CD.

Echo rates can vary from very, very short to incredibly long and you have control over the number of times your guitar signal is repeated, too. Both control parameters have an enormous influence over your guitar sound. On delay units, the actual rate of delay is measured in milliseconds and the extent of delay available to you varies from unit to unit. This kind of electronic wizardry depends an awful lot on processing power and, like in a computer, this kind of thing costs money. So be prepared for smaller, cheaper units to come with a maximum of one to two seconds delay. This might not sound a lot, but as you'll see, it can get you most places that you want to go!

For the first audio example, let's be really heavy-handedly obvious about everything and give you a single guitar note with a fairly long delay time and plenty of repeats.

| example 7 |
| audio only |

CD Track
30

In the field, as it were, that kind of delay setting is only ever used for special effects, but it tells you basically what a digital delay does. You're far more likely to hear delay times of around 360ms (ie less than half a second) with only two or three repeats when you hear a guitarist play live or on CD. It should be subtle enough for you not to notice it – it's really only there to give the guitar sound a bit of space around it. Here's a guitar with 360ms of delay on it:

example 8 audio only	

CD Track
30

You can still hear the delay pretty clearly, but listen to what happens when we put the echoed guitar in a playing context:

example 9 audio only	

CD Track
30

The effect has now become almost transparent – it's just helping the guitar stand out a little.

Sometimes, you'll hear digital delay used for special effects; you can create rhythms using a delay – this next example is reminiscent of a guitar line you might hear Pink Floyd's David Gilmour play...

example 10 audio only	

CD Track
30

In that last example, I'm not playing half of what you're actually hearing – the effect is neatly filling in all the gaps and giving the illusion of lots of notes playing at once.

You can use a delay unit to play in harmony with yourself, a bit like Queen's Brian May.

example 11 audio only	

CD Track
30

Obviously, I'm only playing one note at a time, but, with the right delay settings, I can make the guitar sound like a whole army of guitarists playing together!

Another popular effect is to use the digital delay on a long setting and fade in chords using your guitar's volume control. This has a beautiful 'overlapping' effect and probably is as close as we can get to imitating an orchestra's string section (without using a guitar synthesiser!).

example 12 audio only

CD Track
30

Funnily enough, the most imaginative use of delay comes from country players. Here, by carefully selecting the right delay and echo rate parameters – and some quite precise playing – you can get the echo unit to make you sound like you're playing almost impossible guitar breaks.

example 13 audio only

CD Track
30

Good, huh? I don't play country, but that last example has always been my favourite digital delay party piece!

There's a whole host of other tricks you can perform with a digital delay – I've only really scratched the surface – but I don't want this section to start sounding like a demonstration in a music shop and so it's probably time to move onto another effect. But before we go, I'll mention another little delay gizmo which is becoming increasingly more and more common with recorded guitar sounds.

Some delay units (usually the 'rack' or studio level devices) come with multi-tap delay. Basically, this means that the unit is capable of giving you several different rates of delay simultaneously. Whereas ordinary, non-tapped delay can make a guitar signal stand out either on stage or on CD, the asymmetry produced by having delay times 'beating' against one another can work wonders.

example 14 audio only

CD Track
30

Flanging

This is an effect which is similar to chorus in many respects and one which seems to have nose-dived out of fashion in recent years. But I think you'll know it when you hear it, so it's still worth mentioning.

Legend has it that it was a studio engineer working on a Beatles record who first discovered flanging. They found that by recording a sound onto two tape players and then playing both back together with one machine playing slightly slower than the other (brought about by placing a weight on the tape spool's flange – hence 'flanging') you could make things sound like this:

| example 15 audio only |

CD Track
31

See what I mean about it sounding quite close to chorus? It's very nearly there, but different and more 'hollow' or 'metallic-sounding' to my ears.

Once again, flanging is used to add an electronic contour to a rhythm part...

| example 16 audio only |

CD Track
31

Phasing

It's almost impossible for most of us to think about phasing without associating it with the 60s and The Small Faces' single 'Itchycoo Park'. It's a very distinctive effect which I suppose you'll either love or hate.

| example 17 audio only |

CD Track
31

Back in the 60s, studio engineers tended to brandish phasing like it was some sort of new sonic weapon and use it on anything that moved. Today, perhaps we're a little more refined!

Phasing units can do tricks too – although pretty useless, ugly sounding tricks, it has to be said! OK – phasers on 'stun'...

| example 18 audio only |

CD Track
31

Ouch!

Rotary speaker

Anyone mind if we talk about keyboard players for a minute? It's organists in particular, in actual fact. You may or may not know that organists used to use speaker cabinets which contained rotating speakers. You could control the actual speed of the rotation, depending on what sort of effect you wanted to produce and, if you've ever been subjected to an evening's entertainment by an organist, you'll have heard the effect for sure.

Now guitarists are notorious for experimenting and one day, one such player wondered what his guitar would sound like if he plugged it through a rotating speaker unit. Probably the most famous example of the resulting sound is on The Beatles' 'While My Guitar Gently Weeps' which features Eric Clapton playing through such a device (although, history remembers that the effect was added long after EC had left the building). It's a very distinctive sound and quite a useful one, too; but it never really caught on because who wants to lug around a rotating speaker cabinet (they were incredibly heavy) when you're only going to use it on one song!

Once again, the digital revolution has come to the rescue and now, quite a few multi-effects units include a rotating speaker simulation. Here's what it sounds like:

example 19
audio only

CD Track
31

Once again, it's not dissimilar from chorus and flanging, but it has some unique characteristics of its own. About the only player who has stuck it out with the mechanical devices (although he uses custom-built units called 'Doppolas') is Pink Floyd's David Gilmour. Used in context, you can hear a subtle difference from chorus...

example 20
audio only

CD Track
31

Tremolo

This particular effect is another which probably 'overlaps' a little with rotary speaker effects. The actual sound produced by using tremolo is probably not what you're thinking – not your fault, it's down to the bright spark who mis-named vibrato units on guitars and called them 'tremolo units'. Just to clarify things once and for all; 'vibrato' is a slight variation in a note's pitch, like you can hear on the CD when we talk about finger vibrato in 'What Special Techniques...'. 'Tremolo' is a variation in a note's volume (as far as we're concerned, anyway. Classical musicians know it as the rapid repetition of a single note – but I think you'll see where the line can be drawn between definitions!).

The best way to explain tremolo, of course, is to let you hear it for yourself.

example 21
audio only

CD Track
31

A few years ago, you couldn't give tremolo units away, the effect was considered very old-fashioned (amps built during the 50s and 60s often had it built in). But, due to the cyclic nature of all things fashion-orientated, tremolo is back with us. It's a great way of making a rhythm part sound a little different...

<table>
<tr><td>*example 22
audio only*</td><td></td></tr>
</table>

CD Track
31

Of course, you can vary the tremolo rate, but basically, what you've already heard is the tremolo pedal's full gamut!

Wah wah

Ever since the late 60s when Clapton and Hendrix raced to be the first to record the sound of a wah wah pedal (and neither won, but that's another story!), guitarists have been playing through wah wah pedals.

The pedal was originally developed to allow guitarists to imitate the sound of a trumpet player using a mute. But I've got to say that I find it almost unbelievable that any guitarist would actually want to imitate a trumpet player... In any case, a wah wah pedal is basically a tone filter (almost like the tone control on a guitar) which you can either open or close with your foot. The wah wah aspect is named after the sound produced (so it's 'onomatopoeic', if you like long words...).

<table>
<tr><td>*example 23
audio only*</td><td></td></tr>
</table>

CD Track
32

In use, the effect is usually fairly subtle...

<table>
<tr><td>*example 24
audio only*</td><td></td></tr>
</table>

CD Track
32

Some 'heavy rock' players tend to use a wah wah pedal as an extra tone control, getting that distinctive 'ooo' vowel sound on their solos.

example 25
audio only

CD Track
32

But I suppose the ultimate wah wah experience could be the way Jimi Hendrix used it on muted strings – check out 'Voodoo Chile (Slight Return)' from the album *Electric Ladyland*. Here's the sort of thing I mean:

example 26
audio only

CD Track
32

Pitch shift

As technology ran away with itself during the 80s, the processing power necessary to fire up some of the more computerised effect units became more and more affordable. This meant that effects like the pitch shifter, previously only available in top-of-the-range studio effects packages, became available to the guitarist on the street.

The way a pitch shifter works is a bit scientific, but bear with me. The guitar's signal is sampled, or electronically 'cloned', turned into digital data, its pitch altered to a pre-destined degree (a relatively easy job when everything is reduced to maths), allowing you to play in harmony with yourself...

example 27

CD Track
32

Not everybody's cup of tea, I suspect, but I quite like it! I remember when a pupil of mine bought one and brought it into a lesson for me to fiddle with and when I discovered you could play chords through it and do things like this...

example 28
audio only

CD Track
32

... I went out and bought one myself the following day! It remained a live party piece for a while, but, like so many things, I became tired with the unit's

inflexibility. Once I'd played in octaves (to the dismay of the bass player, whose job felt threatened) just to pep up the odd 'riff' passage...

example 29 audio only	

CD Track
32

... and used a couple of the other harmonic novelties it could produce, which I've outlined

above, I found myself leaving it at home more often.

'Intelligent' pitch shifters

Sometimes, ascribing actual intelligence to a machine is a bit of a contradiction in terms. But the next generation of pitch shifters had one very important trick up their sleeves. If you play a scale

on a regular pitch shifter, the machine will only play notes which are mathematically all the same distance from each other, so you can only play in 'parallel lines':

example 30 audio only	

CD Track
32

As if you needed proof that music and maths are, for the most part, incompatible! The promise made by 'intelligent' pitch shifters was that, given the

necessary musical information in advance, it would keep everything musical. Used with a bit of care and taste you can achieve some pleasing results:

example 31 audio only	

CD Track
32

Much better, I'm sure you'll agree.

The 'pitch shift' effect has never really taken off as a day-to-day affair like, say, the wah wah or chorus unit have. It's fair to say that you have to be

a bit more aware of music's nuts and bolts to get the best out of one, and its effect is still kind of limited, even then. They are, however, bags of fun to sit and play with!

Graphic eq

This isn't really an effect, as such. But it's available in the guise of a regular effects unit and sometimes its use is down the same general road – so I thought it might be worth mentioning.

Just to make sure things don't reach technical overload, let's begin with a couple of definitions. Firstly 'eq' is a sort of blanket term which means, loosely speaking, 'tone control'. You're probably quite familiar with the treble and bass controls on a domestic hi-fi and have probably seen something very similar on your guitar amplifier, too. Which means that you might be familiar with the effect these controls have on the music (or guitar) that you're listening to. A treble control will have an effect over a certain range of frequencies, boosting or cutting them to taste, and so too will the bass control. A graphic eq has far greater effect over the guitar's frequency range, meaning that you have far more control over the tonal mechanics of your sound.

A graphic eq will normally have a series of sliders which boost or cut certain frequencies in the guitar's tonal spectrum. Once you've set it up, you can switch it in and out like any other pedal, giving you the opportunity to switch between two distinctly different guitar sounds at the flick of a well-aimed toe. But a lot of players will use a graphic to boost their guitar signal, using it as 'another stage of gain' as your guitar signal travels ampwards. This can have the effect of bringing the guitar up in volume for a solo, without going the whole hog and using a gain or distortion unit.

The difference may appear at first to be a subtle one, and it's not an effect you'll find at the top of many players' shopping lists, but it can make a real difference, if you're looking for a way of giving your guitar another 'voice'.

example 32
audio only

CD Track
32

Multi-effects patches

As I've already mentioned, multi-effects units are rife in the market at present. The philosophy is a simple one; put five or six effects in a single unit, add some programmability and a few flashing LEDs and guitarists everywhere will love you for ever! Actually, there are a few hidden benefits here which are certainly worth a few sentences...

If you've got to the point where not one, not two but three or more effects are important to you, it would definitely be worth checking out some of the multi-effects units on the market. For a start, multi units are neater on stage and save you having to 'daisy chain' effects together using guitar cable (the potential for tripping over such set-ups has got to be taken into consideration, too!). Secondly, the order in which you wire effects together can make an amazing difference to the overall sound and so, in a multi-effect, you can be fairly sure that it's all been done the right way round. Thirdly, effect for effect, multi-effects units are probably cheaper to buy – a sort of 'buy six for the price of four' type of deal.

In any case, it's pretty certain that you are going to be using more than one effect at once at one time or another and so I thought we'd just consider a couple or guitar sounds which contain a fairly thick layer of 'effects topping'!

example 33
audio only

CD Track
33

*example 34
audio only*

CD Track
33

*example 35
audio only*

CD Track
33

Guitar to MIDI

This doesn't really belong under the heading 'effect' either. For a number of years, guitarists have been trying to interface their instruments with computers and synthesisers with a varying degree of success. The major problem is that a guitar doesn't speak the same language as a synth, making any such link-up nigh on impossible. The breakthrough came when the first guitar to MIDI interfaces began to slip onto the market. In the main, these comprise special, six-channel (or 'hexaphonic' to use the accepted terminology) guitar pick-ups which you fix to the guitar. Why six-way? In order for the right information to get through to all the right places, we have to look at each string individually, meaning we're stuck with six independent signal sources.

After being picked up by the 'hex' pick-up, the guitar signal is converted to a digital MIDI signal via a special conversion process and then, most of the work is done; your guitar is now speaking the correct language and giving a computer or synthesiser the right digital instructions for it to do its job.

So, hypothetically speaking, you are using your guitar to control a synthesiser's voices and you can make the same sounds that a keyboard player would use. Suddenly, you've gone from being a guitar player into a whole new sonic ball game. You can strum choirs and orchestras, flutes and pianos...

Sounds rather romantic, doesn't it and you're probably wondering why, if it's so darned simple,

every guitarist isn't interfacing him or herself crazy. Well, there are a couple of reasons why: one, the kind of technology we're talking about here is at least as expensive as buying yourself another guitar – and it won't sound too good through your guitar amp, either. So, if you follow the guitar synth path through to even a fairly modest conclusion, you'll be shelling out some big bucks. Secondly, the technology that converts your guitar into this new platform of possibility isn't as flexible as it would be from a keyboard.

For a start, the guitar pitch to digital signal process takes a few milliseconds and so a guitarist who is used to instant response from his instrument has got to get used to a whole new 'feel' to his instrument. Secondly, a guitar is still a guitar, even if it's been plugged through a whole shedload of very clever electronics and so you can expect to do rather a lot of adapting, both physically and stylistically, before the whole deal really becomes practical.

It sounds like I'm trying to put you off and I'm not! I find the whole thing fascinating and, being a frustrated keyboard player, have invested in the necessary technology to place my guitar in the digital domain. But I've never used a guitar synth on stage; I've just 'tinkered' at home and a little bit in a studio situation.

Anyway, just for the record, this is what you can do with a guitar pretending to be a keyboard... (Note that all the sounds in the following example were produced on a single guitar – no overdubs!)

*example 36
audio only*

CD Track
34

You can do even more with a computer!

In this age where computers are considered to be portals to the infinite (ahem), more and more processing, recording, editing and so on is being performed in recording studios 'on screen'. Most CDs you hear these days have never been anywhere near recording tape, either; which makes it all the more surprising that guitarists tend to look backwards for their chosen technology. We like guitars and amps from a bygone era simply because nobody has really invented anything since which sounds any better. But the two technologies sit side by side in an amiable sort of way...

That's effects, then. You either love them or hate them, but I'll bet that you end up buying one or two. Although they're not what you might refer to as wholesale 'musical' accessories, they've been part of the guitar vocabulary now for quite a while and there's probably no escaping them!

intro to part two

Welcome to part two. This is where the work really starts and we'll soon be looking at what you'll need for your ten minutes a day in the guitar gym!

Guitar teachers are always being asked by pupils, 'How long should I practise every day?' and most will agree that *any* amount of time a pupil spends with a guitar in his hands is valuable. The problem is trying to get them to practise the right things! Guitarists are inveterate 'noodlers'; we all do it. We sit with a guitar, play everything we know – all the favourite licks and a couple of songs we've sort of half-learned. Then we put down the guitar and tell ourselves that we've done a decent bit of practice!

I've found that I can get people to practise more positively by giving them a series of graduated exercises and actually limiting the time they spend doing them. It's like a bargain or pact; you can do anything you want after you've done this – and it'll only take you ten minutes. Fair deal?

The exercises have a subliminal effect; they are so designed that nothing is impossible to start with and everything follows on logically and progressively. Even with just a ten-minute daily investment on the pupil's part, progress is practically guaranteed.

I once had a pupil who doubted the system's effectiveness after doing it for several months. I used to keep a record of when pupils started a new phase or regimen and so I turned the page back and said, 'OK, play that.' He played what was in front of him perfectly. I said, 'You couldn't

play that eight weeks ago...' and he was amazed! He had been so close to what he was doing, he hadn't noticed that he was progressing at an even rate. This is why it's important to keep your own records of where you've got to and what you've managed to cover and achieve so far. We all need notches, benchmarks or whatever to keep us going, after all.

Apart from the Canadian Air Force, my other inspiration for putting this system together was reading the biography of a famous classical guitarist. Back in the 1940s, he was faced with doing his National Service, as was every young man in Britain at the time. This meant that he would have to curtail his extensive practice routine somewhat severely. He was aware that he couldn't afford to stop practising altogether because, obviously, he would lose so much ground and it would take ages to make good all the time he had lost. He thought that, whatever his duties entailed whilst doing his service, he was sure to have 40 minutes or so each day he could call his own. So he devised a practice routine which comprised exercises exclusively; his thoughts were that if this routine allowed him to 'tread water' for the duration, he would find it easier to continue his studies afterwards.

So, he duly practised every day for all the time he was on National Service, still a little worried about the ground he might be losing. At the end of his service, he returned to his studies full-time – and found that his technique had actually improved! He was actually a far better musician than before inasmuch as he was capable of playing so much more.

Convinced? I was. I began to think how I could fit a great deal of valuable information into the shortest possible time in such a way that technical advances were guaranteed but nothing became too laborious along the way. That way, pupils could get on with the serious business of having fun with the instrument!

how to stay out of casualty

I used to joke with my pupils that there was a ward named after me in the local hospital which was full of pupils who had developed bad practice habits and suffered from tendonitis and repetitive strain injury as a result. Looking back, it was probably a bad joke to make – RSI is not a laughing matter. But I was merely trying to provide cautionary advice on some of the dangers facing guitarists who 'overdo it' while they practise. I feel I must spend some time pointing out how to avoid physical problems arising from playing guitar. After all, we're about to set off on a course of exercises which are designed to have gentle and beneficial effects and I'd hate to think I was innocently responsible for someone getting hurt!

The first piece of advice is probably the most obvious; if you've had any recent problems in your wrists, hands, fingers – or even back (good posture is vital), then take some time to get medical advice first. The exercises here are very gradual and, under normal circumstances, would not put anyone under unacceptable or dangerous levels of stress or strain. You're hardly guinea pigs, after all; everything you see here has been previously tested on humans...

I'm not going to turn this chapter into a medical treatise on music-related disorders, but it will certainly help a great deal of people stay out of trouble and stop cluttering up the doctor's surgery if we consider a few simple facts. The reason why I'm taking this so seriously is that surveys amongst musicians continue to reveal that a staggering 50% suffer some sort of pain or discomfort through the simple means of just doing their job.

It's tempting to think that it must be only sportsmen or athletes who are prone to strain, but this just isn't the case. Just consider for a few moments exactly what is required of your arms, wrists and fingers when you play guitar. Look at the way the left hand is positioned – the body just wasn't designed with the guitar in mind. We've had to adapt ourselves and the instrument and ended up with a compromise which works reasonably well as long as a little advice is heeded.

If you cast your mind back to human biology lessons, you'll remember that movement in the hands is brought about by a combination of bones, joints, muscle, tendons and nerves. The muscle is connected to the bone via tendons at each end. When the muscle contracts, at a signal sent from the brain via the nerve, movement is produced. Sounds simple enough, doesn't it? But if the movement is repetitive and wildly uncontrolled, things can sometimes go horribly wrong. Simply put, it's inappropriate use and poor technique that usually causes the problems. What's more, the damage that can be done in this area is often brought on over a significant period of time and so it may be some time before symptoms are treated seriously by the hapless musician who might not notice or take heed of the various warning signs – and, like most medical conditions, the longer you leave it before taking action, the worse it can potentially get.

You've probably heard of tendonitis or carpal tunnel syndrome, the former being caused by excessive stress on muscles and tendons, the latter being compression of the median nerve which is important for sensation and movement in the hand. Both are seriously bad news for guitarists – players have had to stop playing in the severest cases – and it's not always at the top pro end of the guitar playing pile where problems occur. Enthusiastic amateurs are equally as likely to find themselves in trouble.

So, after the horror stories, let's look at a few ways we can all stay fit and healthy strummers, shall we?

Position

So many guitar students get this bit wrong. I'm as guilty of slouching on a sofa with a guitar on my lap as the next man, but it's not on if you're intending to do some serious practising. If you're leaning back, with your back almost crescent-shaped, hunched over the instrument, you might think you look like a real rock'n'roll dude – but you'd be investing in your body's quiet enjoyment of life and almost maintenance-free running if you make sure that your practice posture is not putting unnecessary strain on other parts of your body.

Keep your wrists as straight as possible and try to avoid 'tensing up'. You'll play a heck of a lot better with little or no tension in your arms, hands and fingers.

It's mainly a matter of common sense just to make sure that you're in a comfortable but workmanlike position when you practise. This all fits in with my plea to make some special provisions for yourself; try to go somewhere quiet, away from distractions and so on. But make sure you're comfortable, OK?

Try to choose a chair which offers good back support and change position every so often, to stop things from 'seizing up'. Most importantly, relax.

Location

Avoid extremes of temperature. Obviously you're not going to go outside and try to practise in the garden shed in the dead of winter... are you? Seriously, cold fingers are not happy fingers and furnace-like heat doesn't do them any good either. As with all things, a little moderation goes a long way.

Warm-up

Whatever you do, whether it's the practice routine outlined in this book or one of your own, make sure you spend a little time 'warming up'. The first exercise in the ten-minute workout is designed to help the fingers 'wake up' slowly and sensibly. Think of your hands as athletes; you wouldn't whip off your tracksuit and bolt off for a 100-metre sprint without a little preparation and so don't expect your hands to want to either!

Relax

Not such a tall order in the practice room, but in front of an audience many players complain that they feel themselves tensing up. The truth is, by introducing tension into your hands, you're not only putting yourself in the way of some of the music-related disorders mentioned above, but it will affect the flexibility of your hands, meaning you're going to start playing badly.

Be conscious of the need to relax. Tell yourself occasionally to 'chill out'. If you get incredibly tense in a performing situation, you may need to seek guidance from a therapist. Oh, and alcohol isn't a good way to relax before a gig! I've been backstage with bands where alcohol is actually banned in the dressing rooms before a show – a lot of this Jack Daniels and 'I'll sleep when I'm dead' routine is put on for the public. Trust me, I'm a journalist...

Take breaks

The ten-minute workout allows for breaks between the different exercises, but if you continue playing or practising afterwards, build in some breaks for yourself. Never play for any longer than forty minutes without taking a break; your concentration diminishes quite quickly over a relatively short period of time and something that started off as a positive learning process ends up as mindless repetition. You make more mistakes if your concentration fails, too.

Breathe

I was amazed when I was given this advice the first time. 'Don't forget to breathe!' someone said. I thought, 'Well I've got this far without forgetting and so I think I can trust my body's autopilot by now...' But I was missing the point. Later on, I actually found myself holding my breath when I was trying to play something difficult, or playing a scale against the clock. And what happens when we hold our breath? Something about starving the brain of oxygen ring any bells? Even for what appears to be a short period of time can have a cumulative effect if you keep doing it and this will affect your concentration, too. So breathe, OK?

Buy a pair of gloves

I can't remember who told me this, but going out in the cold when you've either just finished practising or playing a gig with hot, stretched muscles is an invitation for all sorts of problems. That's one of the reasons you see athletes don tracksuits and why they wrap marathon runners in silver foil.

Apart from that, gloves protect your hands from all sorts of other damage, too.

After a break...

If you've had to stop practising for a while for any reason, such as an illness or holiday, don't expect your hands to be too willing to start back where you left off. You have to give them a while (probably a few days, depending on how long you were 'away') before you can expect them to get back up to speed.

If it's any help, a famous jazz guitarist once told me that, even if he didn't practise for ages,

he knew he was always within a few weeks of returning to his peak. You can see that there are a great many similarities between musicians and athletes, can't you?

Buy a music stand

I know so many people who try to follow music in either books or magazines by placing it on the floor and craning their necks (not to mention straining their eyes) to read it. Music stands are an invaluable practice aid; you can place your study material in direct line-of-sight so you don't have to suffer awkward positions to read it. I usually recommend that people place their music stands slightly to their left so that the business of looking from music to left hand is minimised.

You might find that buying a music stand will have a slight psychological effect too by sheer virtue of the fact that it looks and feels more professional. Let's face it, we need all the help we can get!

Invest in a good guitar strap

When you take your guitar out of its case it might feel as light as a feather, but after a while it's going to feel like a ton of bricks if you've got a thin, unpadded strap. Heavy guitars can cause problems, so spread the weight and stress on your shoulder with a good, thick strap.

Don't adjust your guitar strap so that your playing position puts any unnecessary stresses or strains on you whilst performing. I know it's meant to look dead cool to have a Les Paul slung low around your knees, but it's not doing you any good!

When using a strap, you should adjust it so that everything is easily within reach and that it approximates, as closely as possible, the position in which you practise.

The best advice I can offer on the subject of staying healthy is probably the most straightforward – and, sadly, the most often ignored. If, at any time during playing, you experience any pain or discomfort, STOP

PLAYING! Take a break, you might have just been overdoing things. The warning signs are: pain, stiffness, numbness, aching, tingling and loss of control. Obviously, the most common symptom is wrist pain – this is not a normal part of playing and, as they say on all good medicine bottles, if symptoms persist, go and see a doctor straight away. If he confesses to being unfamiliar with musical-related injuries, ask to be referred to a specialist.

hit the charts

This section represents the real core of what this book's all about. I hope you've read the chapters in part one and I hope too that I've managed to clear up any of the things which puzzle you about the guitar.

More importantly, I trust you've read the chapter on avoiding RSI and other practice-related ailments - I don't want any casualties!

So what are we gong to do? How are we going to make a start?

The Exercises

The exercises have been split into six 'charts' and, not surprisingly, you're expected to start on 'Chart One'. On each chart, you'll find a table which has been split into twelve graduated sections, marked 'D-' to 'A+'. You start at 'D-' and perform each of the chart's exercises the number of times shown.

LEVEL	EX 1	EX 2	EX 3	EX 4	EX 5
A+	30	28	26	36	100
A	28	26	24	33	95
A-	26	24	22	30	90
B+	24	21	20	26	85
B	22	19	17	23	80
B-	20	17	15	20	70
C+	17	15	13	18	60
C	15	12	11	15	50
C-	12	10	8	11	40
D+	10	7	6	9	30
D	7	5	4	6	20
D-	5	3	3	4	10

On the above chart, you would be expected to repeat exercise one five times within two minutes, exercise two three times and so on until you've completed that level (ie five exercises, two minutes each). After a few days - and I would recommend at least three days spent per level - you move up to 'D', where you would perform exercise one seven times in two minutes, exercise two five times and so on - get the picture?

Eventually, probably after a few weeks, you will reach level 'A+' where you will be performing exercise one 30 times, still keeping within the two minute time limit. Now you should start to see exactly *how* you will progress - the exercises don't become more difficult, you just have to play them faster to meet the time requirement. Clever, huh? Thank you, Canadian Air Force!

When you can complete all the exercises at the top of the chart within two minutes (with *no* mistakes!) you can move on to the next, starting once again at the 'D-' level and gradually working upwards.

As each chart progresses, the exercises become more involved and more difficult. At the beginning of each chart, you'll find that you can rest a little while you acclimatise yourself to the new exercises (this factor has been built-in in all the 'D-' levels).

So what's the thinking behind each exercise?

One

The first exercise in all the charts is designed as a warm-up routine to gently stretch your left hand, very much in the way an athlete would perform a few stretches before running in a race. It comprises a series of chord shapes which you must change between and, as you progress up the charts, I've added more shapes to bring all the fingers into play.

This is a very old warm-up exercise which has been around for ages. I first discovered it during the 70s and it's been with me ever since.

Two

The second exercise is arpeggio-based and is intended not only as a cross-string picking workout for the right hand, but an ear-training device, too. Once you get used to hearing it, I encourage you to hum along as you play it. Remember that training your fingers up to cope with all these fretboard gymnastics is half the job; getting some musical information whacked into the brain is no less important! As you progress through the charts, the arpeggios change to incorporate different chord configurations - you'll be surprised what these will do for your chord perception.

Three

You didn't think you were going to be able to get away without playing some scales did you? Once again, the emphasis here is not only on co-ordinating your left and right hands and get them working out in perfect sync, but to introduce the ear to these vital musical cornerstones. You'll be recommended to hum or sing along with this section of the workout, too, for the same reason as before; this information must reside in both the brain and fingers if it's going to do you the most good.

Four

This is where another important factor in guitar playing is addressed - stamina-building. There's no doubt that, whatever level your guitar playing reaches, you're going to be relying on stamina a lot of the time if you're going to avoid early fatigue. If you've ever played for quite a long time, playing perhaps a chord arrangement over and over, you find that your hand will become tired quite quickly. This particular series of exercises is aimed at increasing the level of stamina in both hands so that you tire less easily. They build up strength and co-ordination at the same time (as well as further subtle ear-training along the way for good measure!).

Five

This is really the focal point of the daily workout. All the exercises in this section are chromatic, starting with just three notes picked consecutively over and over (good for co-ordination, stamina and so on) until, by chart six, you're playing a complete chromatic scale over six strings - and singing along, too. In the mean time, you've also travelled all over the fretboard, meaning that you've explored and experienced the variety of stretches involved in so doing. There's a big difference between playing around the fifteenth fret and the third (try it!).

The chromatic scale's importance in music cannot and should not be underestimated; it is the 'mother scale' from which all other scales are derived. Complete mastery of the chromatic scale, both from a physical and mental point of view, gives the student a sort of 'access all areas' pass to music's inner core. I've found so many times that the expert handling of music's smallest item of currency - the semitone - is the closest a guitarist can get to a 'cure-all' or 'magic bullet' from the point of view of ear-training and general fretboard management.

In order to make your progress through the charts as smooth as possible, here are a few guidelines...

Choose the right surroundings

Domestic arrangements being what they are, it's difficult to select a quiet area in which to practice.

But as much peace and quiet as possible is the order of the day; don't permit yourself any distractions. The TV is absolute poison to the concentration and even the most hardened telly-addict can find ten minutes of 'down-time' in which to work out...

Start at the beginning

It may seem obvious to make this sort of request, but all the exercises are designed to have a cumulative effect and you're only going to get maximum benefit by starting at the beginning and working through. Even if something seems too easy, it doesn't matter - things are going to get tough pretty quickly and you'll definitely feel the workout's bite before too long!

Turn the routine into a habit

If you can, try to do the workout at the same time every day and discipline yourself not to take a day off! This way, it will develop into a habit quickly and you'll feel a lot more positive about making steady progress.

Spend exactly the right amount of time on each exercise

If you find things very easy and manageable, don't be tempted to pass over it and get on with the next section. It's all doing you good! Similarly, if you find something too hard to complete in the given time, you've moved on too quickly and should take a few backward steps in the chart until things ease up a little.

Do the exercises in the right order

Everything in the charts has been placed in the order you see them for a reason and so doing them backwards just for a change isn't going to have the same effect!

Never be tempted to move on too fast

I'm really going to ram this one home - only move onto the next level when you feel completely happy that you can complete all the exercises in the given time with no problems. That means everything should be note-perfect and deadly accurate before you proceed upwards.

Read the instructions

Make sure you read the instructions and understand what each exercise entails. Practising an exercise wrongly will only mean you've got to go back later on and mop up the mess! Check the CD to make sure you've got things clear in your head.

Lay-offs

If you have to stop the routine for a while due to holidays or illness, backtrack a little - don't try to begin again where you left off. Let the hands work at a slightly lower level for a while and then continue as before.

Finish the course

As with any exercise regime, this workout will become addictive after a while, but it will only have its full effect if you go through to the end.

There is nothing here which requires Olympic standards of guitar proficiency to master; everyone should be capable of doing everything. Later on, when you customise a practice routine of your own, you can head for as much of a technical facility as you want. These exercises are a good platform from which to set off in any direction you choose.

Don't expect to see instant results

All the exercises are graded so that your skills develop gradually and naturally, but the effects will only make themselves obvious in the fullness of time. It won't be something you can measure with a ruler!

Stay alert!

Listen carefully to what you're playing and try to sing along with at least the scale and arpeggio exercises. The exercises are designed to put information into your ears as well as your hands.

Extra time?

If you've got more than ten minutes to spare, don't repeat any of the exercises, work on something else - a song you've been trying to learn, or a technique you need to develop.

Before we start looking at the basic outline of the exercises themselves, we've time for one more 'frequently asked question' which I know you're dying to have answered...

So How Long's This Going To Take?

Everyone progresses at a slightly different rate. If ever you've been in a classroom situation, you'll know this to be true. So there is no way that I can predict a timescale with any reasonable degree of accuracy. But, always one to stick my neck out and take a few shots in the dark (and mix metaphors, apparently) I would estimate that you're probably looking at around four to six months to cover all the charts. But! There are going to be some who whiz through things on streamlined wings and others who take far longer. But it doesn't matter! Both the speedy and the slow will gain the same

sort of benefits from completing the course - they've got to, if you think about it.

What Now?

So what happens when you've passed the winning post at the end of your guitar workout marathon? Well, for a start, you're very welcome to take elements contained within the workout and continue working with them. It's always wise to include some familiar elements within any new practice routine you start. There's little doubt that you will find that your technical proficiency on the instrument is running at quite a satisfactory level (if not, you've skipped a lot of the exercises because you allowed yourself to become impatient - shame on you; it's only ten minutes a day).

You should find that your ear has developed a musical insight of its own, too and good skill in both these areas will unlock so many doors in your musical endeavours. There are certain to be areas where a few problems remain, but never fear, we've all got blind spots and it's really only a case of isolating these weak areas and working on them.

Go and take a look at the 'DIY Basics' chapter and see what you ought to be getting up to next!

chart one

Here we go, then; the first day at school! Read all the instructions carefully, look at the diagrams and tab and make the occasional double check that you're doing everything right. It's a real hassle, having to take some backward steps to correct something which could have been going right all along with a little care!

Don't be too surprised if you complete all the exercises well within the ten minutes for a while – you'll still benefit from them in exactly the same way. On the other hand, if you find that you're struggling to complete all the tasks within the allotted timescale, don't be concerned; you'll soon find that you speed up enough to start spiralling upwards. Think of it like a board game; sometimes it takes ages to throw a six and start the game – it's a little like that.

Don't forget to make a note of the date when you move up the chart as it gives you a chance to take a real measure of your progress. Don't rush things, either. Even if the first few stages seem really easy, spend at least three or four days on each level before moving up – this way, you'll be taking up the slack at a comfortable pace before the real work starts a little later on.

In between each exercise, allow yourself a little break before continuing. You may find that you need to rest your hand in the middle of certain exercises, too, in which case, go ahead. This is not a military training camp with a cruel Drill Sgt (with a heart of gold) barking at you and calling you a 'wuss' because you're tired. As your stamina increases, the need to take breaks will lessen, but remember that 'no pain, no gain' is all very well, but doesn't apply here! (If you're in any doubt as to why, read the chapter on staying out of casualty again.)

When you're completely sure that you can finish all the exercises within the allotted time and that everything is working well, with no fluffs or foul-ups, the proceed to the next chart and series of tasks.

LEVEL	EX 1	EX 2	EX 3	EX 4	EX 5
A+	30	28	26	36	100
A	28	26	24	33	95
A-	26	24	22	30	90
B+	24	21	20	26	85
B	22	19	17	23	80
B-	20	17	15	20	70
C+	17	15	13	18	60
C	15	12	11	15	50
C-	12	10	8	11	40
D+	10	7	6	9	30
D	7	5	4	6	20
D-	5	3	3	4	10

Exercise One   *2 minutes max*

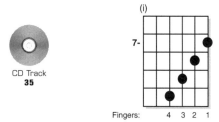

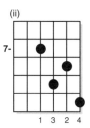

CD Track
35

Look at the two chord shapes above: in this exercise, all you have to do is change between them. Start with the first finger on the seventh fret; the spacing of the frets in this area is quite gentle and your left hand may not be used to spanning 'one finger per fret' straight away.

Basically, you're just moving fingers one and four while the middle two fingers remain static. Aim to complete the changeover in a single movement – don't move the first and fourth fingers one after the other.

Exercise Two   *2 minutes max*

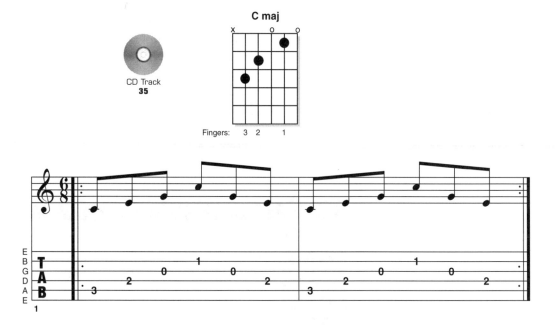

Study the diagram above. You probably recognise the chord shape, but it makes a handy arpeggio, too, as all the notes are in the right order (ie root, third, fifth, root). Hold the chord down with the left hand and employ strict alternate picking with the right.

Once you are used to the sound and feel of this exercise, sing along (or hum, I really don't mind). This should become more and more possible as you progress up the chart because you will be so familiar with the sound you are making – maybe even being able to anticipate it (ie hearing the notes before you play them).

Exercise Three   *2 minutes max*

CD Track
35

This is the first in our series of scales and, as in the last exercise, it's partly physical and partly an ear training exercise. Remember that the major scale is by far the most common in music and so having it set as a template both on the fretboard and in the head

as vital points of reference is incredibly important. Once again, the position is going to look familiar, but working across the strings in series may be still a little unfamiliar. Apply strict alternate picking and aim for 100% clarity at all times.

Exercise Four   *2 minutes max*

CD Track
35

This is the first exercise which may not sound as if it contains any musical 'data' at all. In fact, it does; you're playing minor thirds across two strings – and learning to recognise that intervals will do you some good! But the mainstay of this particular part

of the workout is that it's like a tongue-twister for the right and left hands. It's a puzzle for you to solve which will set up your co-ordination skills in such a way as to provide a solid foundation on which later exercises will build.

Exercise Five   *2 minutes max*

CD Track
35

Don't let the fact that we're only dealing with three notes and three fingers here on a single string mislead you into thinking this exercise is at all 'easy'. At this point in the workout, your hands, wrists and fingers should be loosened up and working well and the gentle 'push' we're going to apply here is where progress will be made.

It might seem that performing this exercise 100 times in two minutes calls for a bit of speed, but it actually means that you have 1.2 seconds to complete each complete cycle – that's less than 60 beats per minute on a metronome. Don't rush – this is more about endurance than it is speed.

chart two

You'll probably notice that these exercises have increased in difficulty a fair deal since we left chart one. Don't be put off; just check out the number of times you have to repeat each exercise within the given time. You start with a little holiday whilst you familiarise yourself with new shapes, regimes, etc and then the slope steepens once again.

Most of these exercises are mere extensions of the ones you've just left. Certainly, they still fall into the same sort of category; gentle stretching, ear training, co-ordination, etc.

Once again, read the instructions for each exercise carefully and check yourself regularly to make sure you are sticking to the rules!

LEVEL	EX 1	EX 2	EX 3	EX 4	EX 5
A+	35	30	15	100	100
A	33	27	14	90	90
A-	31	25	13	80	80
B+	29	23	12	70	70
B	27	21	10	60	60
B-	25	19	9	50	50
C+	23	17	8	40	40
C	20	15	7	30	30
C-	17	13	6	20	20
D+	15	11	5	10	15
D	12	9	3	8	10
D-	10	5	2	5	7

Exercise One   *2 minutes max*

This is an extension of the exercise we looked at in the first chart. This time, we're adding another chord shape, so that the exercise now looks like this:

CD Track
36

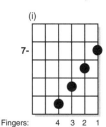

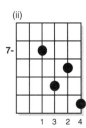

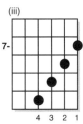

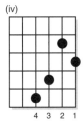

In addition to swapping fingers one and four in position, we're now going to do the same sort of thing for the first and second fingers. The most important thing here is to remember to return to the first position in between the other two.

Exercise Two   *2 minutes max*

CD Track
36

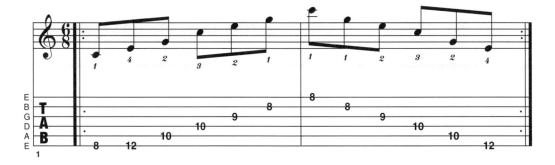

Here we have an arpeggio which covers two octaves instead of only one as before. It means that the fingering is slightly more complex and it will take you a little while to familiarise yourself with it, but you'll soon be playing it like you've known it all your life. Once again, don't be tempted into playing this exercise too fast – even at A+ level you've got four seconds to complete each arpeggio. Use a metronome to 'pace' yourself.

Try to sing along as you play, once you have orientated your fingers on the fretboard. Keep pounding the information into your brain!

Exercise Three   *2 minutes max*

CD Track
36

The scale for this chart is a two-octave G major scale in a closed position (which means it's movable). It's also quite low on the neck which means that there is quite a stretch involved, especially if you are not used to using your fourth finger too much.

Be very strict with yourself over the alternate picking idea; if this sort of thing isn't addressed in the early days, it takes a great deal of time to go back and correct later on.

Make sure every note is of equal volume and try to keep your picking as even as possible (use a metronome if you have one). Sing along so that the ear's appreciation of the major scale is good and solid.

Exercise Four   *2 minutes max*

CD Track
36

Another finger-twister! This exercise will do wonders for your picking accuracy, but it will also encourage you to look seriously at your muting technique. Guitar parts that call for this kind of rapid picking technique are not uncommon, but unless you have some sort of muting facility, the result will turn out to be an unintelligible mess.

Lay the fleshy edge of your right hand palm down on the strings while you pick and you'll find that everything starts to become clear. Keep the picking strictly alternate, too.

Exercise Five   *2 minutes max*

CD Track
36

We're still very much in chromatic territory with this exercise, but this time the fourth finger is brought into play. Also, you are playing the semitones further down the neck to give the hand a little more 'span' than before. Watch your fluency here; there is a big difference between playing this exercise so that it remains crystal clear and badly so that it's a blurry mess. Don't be satisfied until every note sounds as though it's been individually formed.

Don't forget that even 100 times over a two-minute period is only once a beat at a metronome speed of 50 beats per minute. Strive for accuracy, speed will come later.

chart three

Welcome to chart three! By now, your right and left hands should feel like they are working together a lot more than before. Your left hand should be developing nicely with the traditionally weak third and fourth fingers beginning to co-operate with the rest of the hand.

The ten-minutes-a-day routine should have become a habit, too and so you should have no difficulty taking on this new set of exercises – in fact you will doubtless welcome the change...

LEVEL	EX 1	EX 2	EX 3	EX 4	EX 5
A+	40	37	25	40	14
A	37	35	24	37	12
A-	35	33	23	35	10
B+	33	30	22	30	9
B	31	27	20	25	8
B-	29	25	18	22	7
C+	27	22	16	18	6
C	25	20	15	15	5
C-	22	17	13	12	4
D+	19	15	12	10	3
D	15	12	10	7	2
D-	12	10	5	5	1

Exercise One — *2 minutes max*

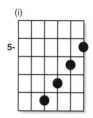
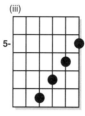
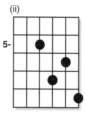

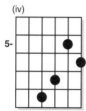
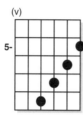
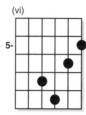

This initial warm-up exercise has now grown another chord shape. We've also moved the whole thing down to the fifth fret so that the stretch increases slightly.

The new shape sees the third and fourth fingers swapping position in addition to the other movements you have performed so far. As before,

it's important that you return to position one in between the changes – consider it the 'home chord'.

As these exercises increase in complexity, remember to take the occasional break if necessary; flex the fingers, let them relax completely and then continue.

Exercise Two — *2 minutes max*

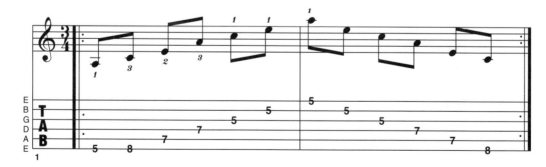

Another arpeggio. This time, it's a minor arpeggio over two octaves. Once you have got the fingering sorted out over the first few times you play it, try singing along as before. Remember that the sound of the minor scale is an important one to

programme into your brain. You'll come across it plenty of times in the future and if both your fingers and brain recognise it, you shouldn't have too much of a problem dealing with it in either respect.

Exercise Three *2 minutes max*

CD Track
37

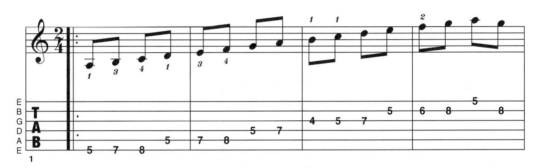

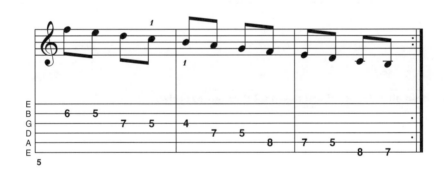

To go along with our minor arpeggio, we've got a minor scale. This is another two-octave scale and you should sing along with this, too, once you've found out where everything fits.

You'll remember from the chapter on scales earlier on in the book I mentioned that there are

no less than three types of minor scale in music's mainstream: the natural, melodic and harmonic. This is the natural minor scale which, without any doubt, wins the prize for being the most used in 'popular' styles of music. Get used to its sound – you'll be meeting it quite often!

Exercise Four   *2 minutes max*

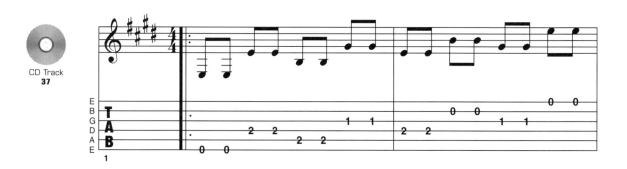

CD Track
37

IMPORTANT: Hold all notes of chord down all through exercise

This exercise, in our series of finger-twisting conundra, is to improve your cross-picking technique. This means that, rather than pick every successive string as you might in an arpeggio, you're picking every other string. A sort of pick one,

miss one idea. It will do wonders for your picking accuracy, which is obviously vitally important for any guitarist or indeed any guitar style.

The important thing here is to start very slowly and only speed up as your confidence increases.

Exercise Five   *2 minutes max*

Still keeping to our chromatic theme, this exercise is similar to the one on the previous chart – it's just that this one moves... It's definitely going to take you a while to acquaint yourself with the mechanics of this particular workout, but once you've set up the initial mechanism, you'll find it's quite a busy, but very rewarding exercise.

chart four

Now that you are halfway through the exercises, things should really be beginning to 'bite'. If you're playing other things outside the ten-minute routine – and I expect you are, the guitar is a difficult instrument to ignore for too long – you will definitely be noticing an increased facility in several areas of your playing. Co-ordination, accuracy and stamina should all have increased tenfold since you started the workout – and things can only get better!

LEVEL	EX 1	EX 2	EX 3	EX 4	EX 5
A+	40	32	30	15	9
A	38	30	28	14	8
A-	36	28	26	13	7
B+	34	26	22	11	6
B	31	25	20	10	6
B-	28	22	18	9	5
C+	25	21	16	7	4
C	23	19	15	6	3
C-	20	17	14	4	3
D+	18	15	12	3	2
D	16	12	10	2	2
D-	14	10	8	1	1

Exercise One   *2 minutes max*

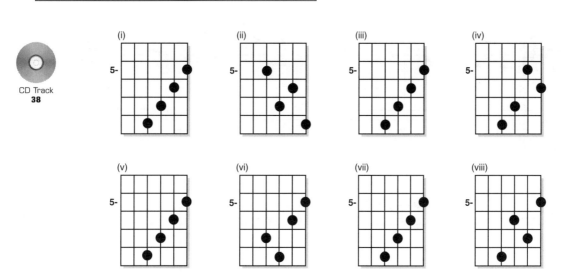

CD Track
38

You probably guessed we were going to add another chord shape to this exercise - and you were right! Now it's the turn of the middle two fingers to swap position on the fretboard and you will find this surprisingly problematic at first. These two fingers don't generally enjoy a lot of independent movement in everyday use (if you're right-handed, that is) and you're probably

going to have a bit of a job getting them to toe the line.

Once you've got it up and running, though, you're going to find that this is an excellent warm-up exercise which you'll want to keep with you all the time. I've used it at gigs just to get my fingers working (one memorable time in the front-of-house gents' loo!).

Exercise Two   *2 minutes max*

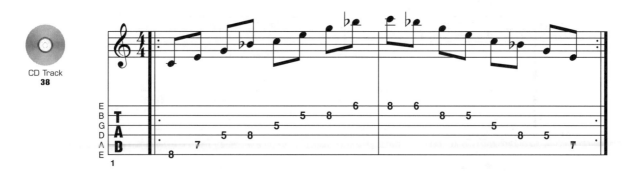

CD Track
38

This arpeggio is a dominant seventh type. You'll notice straight away that it's got more notes in it than either the major or minor did. Where they dealt with the first, third and fifth notes of their respective scales, the dominant seventh arpeggio has four notes – the root, third, fifth and flat

seventh. It's the difference in sound that's important to note, though. So sing along, as before!

By familiarising yourself with the major, minor and dominant chord, arpeggio and scale sounds, you have prepared your ear for a vast amount of what music has to offer.

Exercise Three   *2 minutes max*

We haven't talked too much about modes as yet (although they feature prominently in the third part of this book) but this scale is known as the Mixolydian. Translated back into English, it's a scale which fits dominant chords and is used predominantly in blues, funk and jazz. So it's basically a major scale with a flattened seventh note (in this case, F natural instead of G major's F#). It's a very good sound to include in your 'head vocabulary' and sits side by side with this chart's arpeggio study.

Exercise Four   *2 minutes max*

This probably sounds very dissonant at first hearing, but it's taking your confidence with a plectrum to new heights. We're covering all six strings in a sort of three-strings-at-a-time pattern, backwards and forwards. It calls for considerable co-ordinative skills and will probably take a while to get up and running.

If you can get this exercise up to speed and still keep it crystal clear and note perfect, your picking is coming along nicely.

Once again, a little muting will work wonders with this exercise to ensure that the notes remain distinct.

Exercise Five   *2 minutes max*

CD Track
38

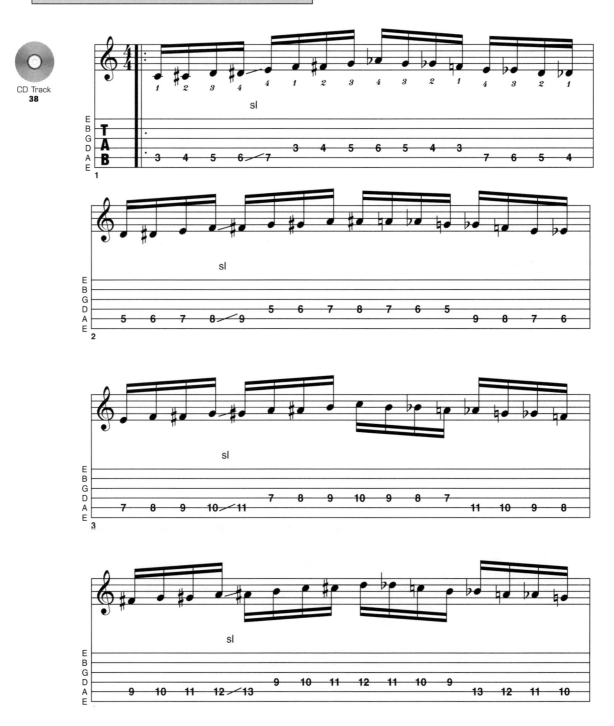

This exercise ought to be accompanied by demonic laughter! We've taken the procedure we started in chart three and added a second string and a slightly different way of climbing up the fretboard. This is the most difficult exercise you have performed so far and so take a great deal of care whilst you're experimenting and getting used to the feel of things. Pay extra special care to the fingerings and take things easy to start with – at the first sign of any discomfort, stop and rest. Nothing here relies on Herculean powers of strength, but we still don't want to rush things.

chart five

The chances are that it is quite some time since you started this workout and I hope things are proceeding nicely. The last two charts represent a sort of 'finishing school' where the final buff is given to the technique which you have accumulated so far. At this point, if you haven't done so before, it might be a good idea to look back over the ground we've covered so far. There will be moments you remember as being infernally tricky which should now be simplicity itself to play. It's a good way to measure your progress especially when you've been working on something for so long – everyone needs benchmarks! Anyway, let's get back to the fun stuff...

LEVEL	EX 1	EX 2	EX 3	EX 4	EX 5
A+	38	15	15	33	15
A	35	14	14	30	14
A-	33	13	13	27	11
B+	30	12	12	25	10
B	27	11	11	23	9
B-	23	10	10	20	8
C+	19	9	9	18	6
C	15	8	7	15	5
C-	13	7	6	13	4
D+	10	5	5	11	3
D	7	3	3	8	2
D-	5	2	2	5	1

Exercise One   *2 minutes max*

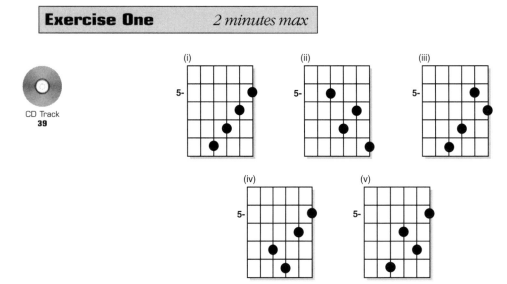

CD Track
39

Surprise! I haven't added another chord shape this time, we're just going to play this exercise in a slightly different way. The main difference is that we're going to stop returning to position one in between each chord shape. This means that you've got to control more than two fingers at once and, at first, you're going to find it a real twister! Part of the reason for this, of course, is because you've got so used to doing the exercise the other way. You've got to break a habit pattern which has been set-up within your hand.

This is going to do wonders for your chord changing capabilities, incidentally.

Exercise Two   *2 minutes max*

CD Track
39

E7   A7   D7   G7

C7   F7   B♭7   E♭7

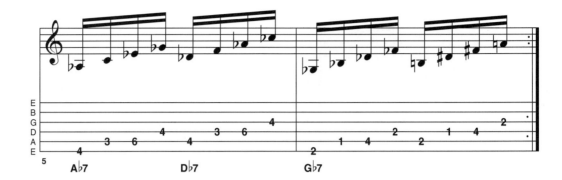

This is a bit different. We've gone from doing whole arpeggios to doing quite a few at once! Here, we're playing dominant seventh arpeggios in the order of the cycle of fourths – which is just a way of saying keys which resolve into each other. There is considerable movement over the fretboard, but it's always the same sort of pattern and so once you've got it up and running, you shouldn't have too much of a problem.

This is another exercise which is designed to convey certain musical information to the brain. Music tends to have certain predictable areas and the order that keys resolve into one another is one of those areas. If you learn to hum along with this exercise, you're teaching yourself much more than just another arpeggio exercise – there's a lot of vital information here, too.

Exercise Three   *2 minutes max*

CD Track
39

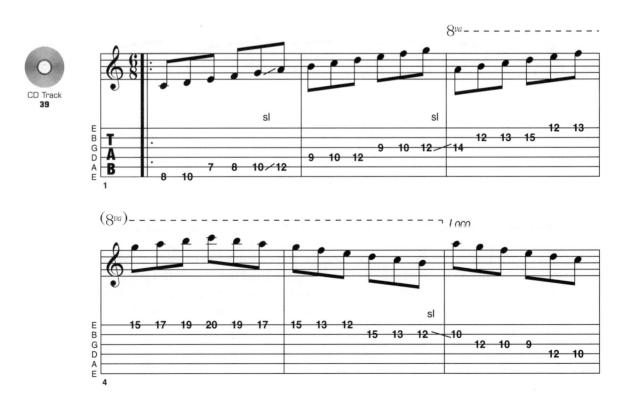

This time, we're returning to the familiar territory of the major scale – it's just that we're going to be covering a lot more ground. This is a three-octave scale, which puts about 90% of the guitar's range at your disposal and involves a couple of fairly tricky position changes along the way. This is a great way of coming to terms with the fretboard and breaking free of single position playing. It also pushes your technique even further to bring much more music well within your own playing horizon. Take care when changing position so that everything remains clear – you shouldn't be able to 'hear' the change at all. It should sound merely like a continuous stream of notes (check the CD if you don't quite see what I mean).

Exercise Four   *2 minutes max*

CD Track
39

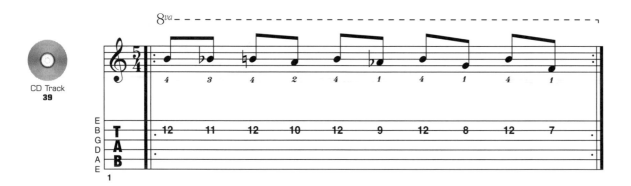

This is an exercise I used to do myself quite a lot. It's not only good for getting the co-ordination between your left and right hands sorted out, but it's another way of increasing the span of the fretting hand quite significantly. It's not absolutely vital to be able to achieve massive stretches with the left hand, but being able to cope with the normal demands placed upon this hand is absolutely vital.

If there is any hint of under-development still in your left hand little finger, this exercise should sort it out. It's a fairly tough one to perform fluently, but once you've addressed the initial 'settling in' with the exercise, you'll find it a very satisfying experience.

Exercise Five   *2 minutes max*

CD Track
39

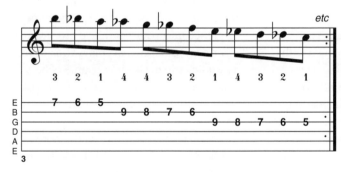

etc

Continue ascending the neck using the same fingering pattern...

Descending

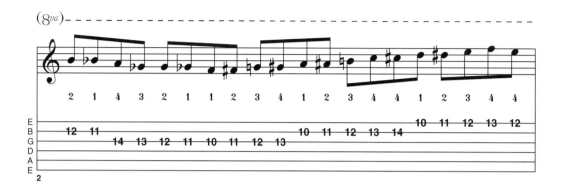

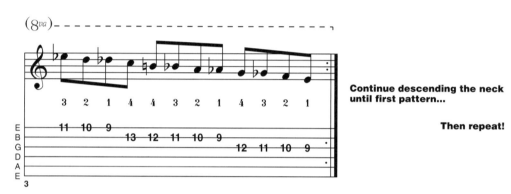

Continue descending the neck until first pattern...

Then repeat!

So far we've been concentrating our chromatic endeavours on the lower strings, but this time we're going to be working over the top three. This is a single octave chromatic scale which moves up the fretboard in its own peculiar little way (please; pay extra attention to the fingering) and you're beginning to cover five frets with four fingers quite competently. This puts the maximum range of notes under the fingers at any single scale position which prepares you for pretty much every eventuality. You're going to cover a fair amount of the neck during this exercise and the way I've written it out relies on you being able to 'programme' a fingering sequence into your head. I've given you a couple of examples of how to play the exercise whilst ascending the neck and a couple of how to descend. Watch your fingers, remember the pattern of the scale – this kind of thing will be really important to you later on.

Once again, make sure all the notes are clear and not blurry or indistinct and check that your alternate picking really *is* alternate!

chart six

If chart one was the first day at school, then you're nearly ready to clear out your locker and say goodbye to matron! We've reached the final slope in our assault on mount technique and the going isn't getting any easier. But, by now, you probably wouldn't want it to anyway.

You should know the drill by now: take a little while to learn the various exercises by heart and then start to increase their frequency within your ten-minute workout. You're nearly there!

LEVEL	EX 1	EX 2	EX 3	EX 4	EX 5
A+	22	23	17	21	20
A	21	21	16	19	19
A-	20	19	15	17	18
B+	18	17	13	16	17
B	16	15	12	15	16
B-	15	13	11	13	14
C+	13	11	9	11	12
C	12	8	8	10	10
C-	10	7	7	8	8
D+	9	5	6	7	6
D	8	3	5	5	4
D-	7	2	3	3	3

Exercise One   *2 minutes max*

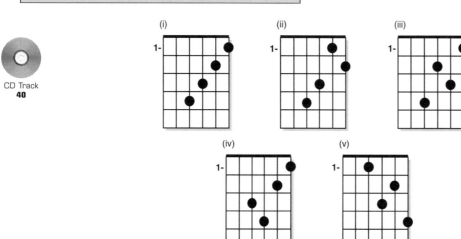

You may have been wondering exactly what curve I was going to throw into this exercise for its grand finale, but, in fact, it's really nothing much. All we've done is altered the order in which you play the chord shapes and relocated them down at the first fret. The latter of these changes is going to make the most difference to you; the left-hand stretch is far more significant than it was. This means that you are more prepared for any rapid chord action down at the first position and that the chord-playing hand is prepared for changing chords over the biggest span it can reasonably be expected to achieve.

I recommend that you keep this exercise in your practice routine after you finish my workout. I haven't found a better one for getting the left hand up and running in the shortest possible time.

Exercise Two   *2 minutes max*

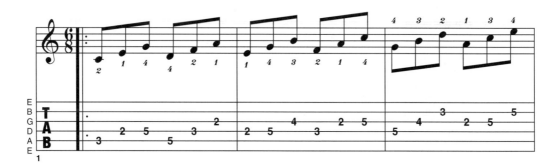

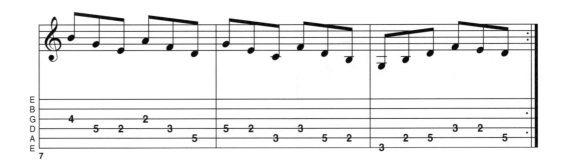

This is another interesting diversion from the straightforward arpeggio theme. Here, we are playing the arpeggios from all the chords within a single key in one compact exercise. (See the chapter 'More About Scales And Chords' for a full explanation of the relationship between chords, arpeggios and scales.)

It is more vital than before that, once you've overcome the initial obstacles thrown up by the

learning process, you familiarise your ear fully with what is going on here. Being able to hear all the arpeggios contained within a single key is a considerable advantage for any musician and so, once again, sing along with these arpeggios as you play them. By doing so, you're building yourself a storehouse of 'internal knowledge' which will be incredibly useful in the future.

Exercise Three   *2 minutes max*

CD Track
40

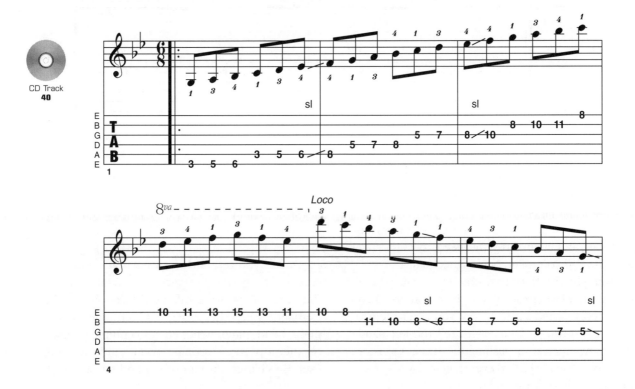

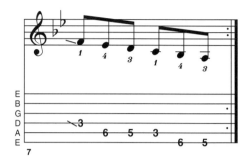

This is another three-octave scale, this time the minor variety. Once again, your ear will learn a lot of information from repeating this exercise, but your fingers will also gain a lot from it, too. If you think that the guitar fretboard spans just under four octaves, you can imagine how much good you are doing yourself by learning an exercise which spans three of them! This probably represents the most you'll have to move around the fretboard in a normal playing situation. After becoming fully competent with this exercise, very little is going to trouble you.

Exercise Four   *2 minutes max*

CD Track
40

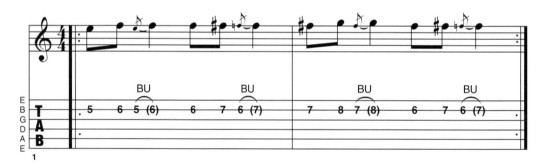

This exercise sounds absolutely terrible if it's played badly and it's definitely the most difficult of our musical 'tongue-twisters'.

It's very similar in design to the chromatic exercises, but it involves the need to master an accurate and controlled bending technique.

You should find that the fact that you're constantly playing the notes which you are then expected to bend up to before you bend them a help. It's down to your ear to tell the left hand fingers when to stop pushing the string. Over- or underbending is a hazard every guitar player knows only too well – both sound pretty awful. And so this exercise should help introduce that vital degree of accuracy into your bending technique.

Take things very slowly to begin with and build up your speed as your confidence and accuracy increase.

Once you're fairly sure that you are consistently performing accurate bends, change the exercise to to a different location on the fretboard. Keep the principle exactly the same – pitch, bend, pitch, bend, etc and confine yourself to the top three strings. You'll find that the exercise changes in nature depending on which string or fret you start on.

Exercise Five — *2 minutes max*

The most important scale in music – every note in the musical alphabet played consecutively – played using all six strings of the guitar. This exercise in some ways represents everything we've been looking at so far. It's a vital ear-training exercise; full command of the chromatic scale is fundamental to all music from the ear's point of view. You're dealing with music's smallest item of currency, after all – the semitone. If your ear can come fully to terms with this interval, practically anything then becomes possible.

The other thing here is, once again, a matter of stretch. The chromatic scale means that you have to play over a span of five frets using four fingers. Once this basic technique is mastered, every note over a two and a half octave span (more than half the guitar's range) will be available to you from a single position. It means that your left hand has assumed the fullest possible control over the fretboard within a single position.

It also calls for accurate co-ordination and picking control, thereby tying virtually everything we've been trying to achieve into a neat, musical knot.

There. You've completed the workout and should find that your fretboard skills have developed nicely. You're ready now to progress onto your own custom practice routine which will point you in the musical direction you want to follow. The 'DIY Basics' chapter which follows will tell you how to put together your own workout, but I hope you continue to look back and explore some of these exercises occasionally. Extend them; change them to suit your own purpose and remember that, unless you constantly challenge yourself on the instrument, you cannot guarantee progress. Create some obstacles and learn to overcome them!

Chapter 12

DIY basics

When you reach the end of the course of exercises in this book, I hope two things will have happened: you'll find that you have developed a considerable technical facility on the guitar which makes a great deal of music well within your grasp. Secondly, I hope you'll be hungry for more! You'll have got into a good habit by having a regimented practice routine and, with a little bit of thought, you will be free to take things further if you wish to. The idea is to build yourself a custom practice routine which deals with things you want to learn or develop. But you'll still need a structure to work to, or the temptation to become a little slack might be just too overwhelming!

This is where some of the information contained in the first part of this book should help you. You might find that you need to develop your knowledge of chords or scales; you might want to learn whole songs or just solos. Whatever you choose, you've already got a distinct advantage of having been 'conditioned' to practise (I could have used the word 'brainwashed', but then I thought of that particular word's sinister overtones...).

Everything in the workout was aiming at one of six essential areas:

Warming Up
Scales
Chords/Arpeggios
Ear Training
Stamina-building

So let's look at those areas one at a time and see what sort of thing you should consider doing in each section.

Warming up

This is probably the most important part of any practice schedule. As we've seen before, you can't expect your hands and fingers to leap into action straight away, they need coaxing. You'll have seen in the workout exercises that a simple, repetitive, gentle stretching exercise will get everything oiled up and working nicely. As to what you actually do in this area, you could do a lot worse than continuing the five chord shapes you've lived with for a while already. It's a good warm-up exercise that's been around for years. But if you yearn for something different, almost literally anything which has a similar effect will do the job. Instead of chords, you might choose something like this:

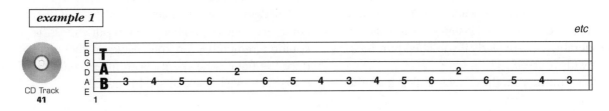

example 1

CD Track
41

You'll be able to tell when everything's loosening up and you're ready for the next stage.

Scales

In the workout section, we looked at only a few scales and, in order to keep my promise and not expose you to anything you didn't need to know just yet, they were quite straightforward. If you want to continue your explorations in this area, you'll find that you're pretty much spoiled for choice.

Your aim is to learn all the common scales in every key. We've already seen that the guitar lends itself to this kind of thing quite nicely. Learn a scale in one key and move it around the fretboard and you've got it!

I've gone into more detail about scales in the final part of this book and dipping into that occasionally will, I hope, provide you with any inspiration for where to go to next for a hit on scales. But, for the time being, nailing all the major and minor scales in both Pentatonic and seven note varieties should be your priority. You've got all the information you need to spread all of the shapes for the majors and minors all over the fretboard – referring back to the chapter on scales in the first part of the book should provide you with everything you need to know.

When I was learning scales, I used to pick a different key for myself every day and play every scale in that particular key. For instance, I might have picked B, so I would play all the five shapes for the major scale in B, followed by the minor and then the two Pentatonic scales. Next day, I'd go somewhere else and repeat the experiment. If you want to keep the ten-minute-a-day regime in place, try to play only one variety of scale every day, but still keep swapping your key centre around.

It might be a case of a lot of map-reading to begin with; lining up root notes on your fretboard chart and looking up the various shapes. But as you progress, you'll need to refer to the charts/diagrams less and less. Your fluency will increase and your instincts will sharpen considerably – particularly if you keep humming along with yourself.

After you've run these four scales into the ground, by all means look for new sound areas to explore. Spend some time with the modes, for example – they're all detailed in part three.

Just tell yourself that every scale you master from both a physical and aural point of view, you're increasing a vital facility for yourself as a musician.

Chords/Arpeggios

There is always work to be done in this area. Once again, check back to the first part on the book for a system of learning chords and once you've exhausted that, look forward to part three for more study.

Consciously build your stock of chords, label and file them away in your head for use in the future.

If, at some point, you become satisfied that your chord vocabulary is really quite sufficient to serve you in your musical endeavours, then extend this part of your practice routine to include learning new chord arrangements. In order to keep yourself on your toes, it's very important that you continually expose yourself to new material, otherwise you'll become stale.

Whichever way round you choose to expand your knowledge in the area of chords, remember your ear has to be spoon-fed with any new information, too. If you come across a chord with which you are unfamiliar, make sure you play it one note at a time to give the ear a chance to latch on to the notes it contains. Play it, then sing it – you'll be doing yourself an unbelievable amount of good this way.

If you ever have trouble memorising a certain chord, there are two tips that I picked up and, used in combination, seem to work every time. One is to write down the troublesome shape and place it somewhere that you're going to see it constantly. The exact positioning is up to you, but I've known people write a chord down on a scrap of paper or one of those self-adhesive notes you see in stores and stick it in the car, on the fridge, by their alarm clocks – almost anywhere. One pupil I had used to put chords he couldn't remember on the inside of the toilet door; he figured he spent about fifteen minutes every day... well, you can see his point!

The other 'aide memoire' is slightly more surprising. Did you know that your fingers have memories, too? I didn't until this trick was proved to me. Play the awkward chord on your guitar and keep your left hand pressed down on the shape. Now, take your right hand and gently press the fingers of the left hand onto the strings gently but firmly, like you were cutting cookie shapes or something. Do it hard enough to leave an impression of the string in each respective fingertip. Take your hand off the fretboard and form the shape again. Anything happened? Did you find that your fingers formed the shape a little more readily this time? Keep repeating the process for a while and you should find that the fingers start 'remembering' the shape by themselves; you've literally left an impression on them.

Now, the chances are that this process is almost entirely psychological, but who cares, as long as it works!

Ear training

Again, checking back at the chapter on ear training in part one of the book should be sufficient fuel for your learning fire to begin with. As long as you do something which inputs some sort of information to your brain every day, you will find that your ability to 'speak the language' increases accordingly. It's the area that most people ignore and yet, as we've seen, it's one of the most important.

You'll be dealing with a great deal of physical data every time you practise, but keep at the back of your mind that this is only half the task at hand – you're merely learning to operate a machine. You have to programme the 'language' into your head, too.

I'll say again that singing everything you play is probably the best way of tying the physical and non-physical elements of learning music together.

Stamina-building

I hardly need to say that, to keep yourself in top physical shape, you need to continue some sort of exercise programme. Having completed the workout will mean that your hands already have a considerable resource to call upon as far as stamina or 'chops' is concerned and it would be a pity to let things slide now.

There are various ways you can keep your physical capacity fully charged. Buy a metronome, play some scales at ever increasing speeds (but easy does it, OK?), construct a few exercises of your own, look back to the exercises in the workout and use some of them – anything. Imagine, once again, that you are an athlete who needs to remain in peak condition and a few minutes a day in the guitar gym is all that's necessary!

Before we leave the subject of your own DIY workout, I'll mention a couple of other points, too.

Try to keep yourself disciplined. I maintain that limiting yourself to a set amount of time to 'work out' every day is best from all points of view. It will keep everything ticking over and, at ten minutes a day, shouldn't ever become a chore. What's more, if ten minutes is all you can spare, you won't feel guilty that you're not spending enough time with the instrument in your hands, because I hope I've proved that, with a little bit of planning, it can easily be sufficient.

There's one more area to look at before we move on...

Guitarists just want to have fun!

Believe it or not, this area of practice is the most overlooked. You've just done a lot of work, now it's time to party! There should always be a point where you can pretend that teacher's gone out of the room and you're free to do whatever you want. Call it carrot and stick philosophy, if you like, but reward yourself with a few minutes of playing anything you want after your practice routine is over. Don't ascribe any seriousness to this section of your practice schedule – school's out, just have fun with your instrument. Bond with that guitar!

That's really about it. There is nothing magical

about making progress on the guitar, all you need is a bit of guidance and a certain amount of self-discipline to follow through. Anyone can become a very good player if they want to badly enough!

now go play a gig!

This chapter assumes that you might at some time want to put all the work you've done honing your skills as a musician to good use and play in front of an audience. I'll leave the exact definition of the word 'audience' to you; it could be family members at a party, it could be with a band at a local pub. Of course, it could turn out to be Madison Square Garden, who knows?

Anyway, this is the equivalent of your mum making sure you've got your bus fare and dinner money (and clean pants on) before you leave for school...

I don't have to tell anyone that playing in front of people is very different from sitting alone playing in private. It really doesn't matter whether the people you're playing to are your best friends or people you've never met, it still puts additional stresses and strains on you – suddenly, you're a performer, not just a guitar player and that's very different, somehow.

So, with all this additional hassle, you want to make the job of actually playing as easy as possible and you can do so by planning ahead. It's common sense that things can go wrong when playing live – although most of the time they don't (I don't want to put anyone off!). By taking a few simple precautions, you can stem the tide of misfortune; I work on one basic principle – you can't take a spare for everything you're going to need, but you'd be well advised to go prepared for the worst.

Here are some basic lessons which experience has taught me in the past...

Buy a guitar case or padded bag

It might sound obvious, but you're going to need something pretty tough to protect your guitar from the rigours of gigging life. But I still see guitarists turning up to play with their precious instrument in a cardboard box (or in one instance, a bin liner!).

A good, sturdy guitar case – and by 'sturdy' I mean one that you wouldn't be afraid to jump on with your guitar inside – might seem an expense you could live without, but it will pay for itself the first time someone blunders into it whilst you're packing up – or worse.

If you're not going to gig often, a padded bag will do nicely. Once again, don't buy a cheap one which offers no protection at all to the instrument inside (or you might as well use a bin liner!). Look carefully and think beforehand how it would stand up to the odd knock or bump.

Buy a guitar stand

Or, if you can't stand the thought of yet further expense, promise yourself that you'll keep your guitar in its case when you're not playing. I've heard about so many accidents that have happened due to no fault on the part of the player concerned and damage to guitars can cost a lot of money to put right.

Consider instrument insurance

This is really only if you are going to find yourself playing regularly. The world of insurance is not an easy one to venture into and musical instrument insurance in particular is not something which every broker will even consider. But it's worth shopping around a bit – instruments do get stolen from even the most vigilant owners and so it's worth taking every precaution or remedial action you can.

Preparation

Another obvious one; make sure you know everything you're going to play well. That's what practice and rehearsals are for and 'nearly' or 'almost' is not good enough. Playing in front of people is quite a distraction to begin with and if you don't know the music well enough, it could be just enough to put you off. It's a fact that most goofs, cock-ups or 'train wrecks' on stage are caused by lack of proper preparation and nothing looks worse, or does more harm to your self-confidence, than making a serious bloomer in front of an audience.

Having said that, don't be overly self-critical. Minor fumbles or the odd missed note will probably never be noticed by the audience and so don't let the fear of making a mistake ruin your enjoyment of playing. Even the very best players make mistakes occasionally.

Don't practise on stage

Following on from the last paragraph, there's a saying amongst musicians that the concert platform is not the place to practise. Don't be tempted to experiment too much to the extent that you might find yourself up a blind alley without the necessary savvy to get yourself back out! You're there to entertain the audience and despite the fact you've heard the guitar part to the song you're playing 1000 times, it's probably their first time and so let them enjoy it!

Arrive at the gig in good time

This is one thing that has become something of a personal crusade of mine. I would rather be early for a gig than have to rush in and set up my gear in a panic. A couple of times I've left it pretty close and arrived with only a few minutes to get my gear and myself in order before going on stage and playing, but it's always been due to traffic or other extenuating circumstances and I've always regretted it.

Give yourself enough time to settle down after humping gear into a venue and plugging in, soundchecking and running through something with the band.

Buy decent guitar leads

Don't be tempted into buying cheap guitar leads, it's just not worth the hassle. They tend to crackle and you do lose signal through them, too, which will affect your sound. The chances are that the jack plugs won't be too securely fastened, either. Guitar cable receives a fair amount of tugging and has to endure a lot of movement even at the most demure gigs and so 'economy' cable is out!

Check your gear regularly

Most of what we take with us to gigs is pretty maintenance-free. As long as you've checked the strings on your guitar aren't getting old and likely to break, there's nothing much else to worry about... or is there? It's a good idea to check the wiring in plugs and plugboards every so often and it's wise to check guitar leads, too. With the latter, make sure everything is crackle-free and fully operational.

Get the details right

Make sure you're well aware in advance of how long you're expected to play for, when you can arrive and unload and if you've got a chance for a soundcheck before the public arrives. Different venues have different ways of operating and so it's unwise to leave anything to chance. You can probably sort all the details out with a single phone call and it's well worth the effort.

Buy a plugboard

You might think that if a venue has live music on a regular basis, the very basic question like the number of available power points in the stage area would have been sorted a long time ago. But this isn't always necessarily the case. I did a gig once where we couldn't find any power in the stage area at all. We were just going to try and find someone to ask, thinking we must have missed something, when the barman told us that when we were ready to play, give him the nod and he'd unplug the juke box! That's right; one socket for the whole band...

The golden rule is to make sure you carry enough sockets for your gear. If you've got an amp and a mains-operated effect, then carry a plugboard with a minimum of two sockets.

Buy a decent road atlas!

I've got lost on my way to gigs plenty of times and so has just about every musician I know. There was one gig where we were playing at a country house miles from anywhere and so I phoned the owner for directions. The actual address was one of those vague, countrified affairs like 'The White House, Little Warton-The-Noze, Snedbury' and didn't really give away any clues to its actual location. He told me that the house was fairly difficult to find, but not to worry because, as they were expecting quite a few guests, they were putting signs up as far back as the main road so that everyone would find their way. I set off a little bit earlier than I perhaps would have done, maybe sensing a problem, and found myself driving around for ages trying to find the signs. At one point, I met the bass player coming in the opposite direction along a quiet country road. We decided to form a convoy and set off again, aware that the clock was ticking away. Eventually we found the house by chance, telling the organiser that we must have missed his signs. 'Oh, I haven't put them up yet,' he told us. Doh!

Keep a diary

Many bands get booked up well in advance and keeping track will be difficult if things aren't organised properly. Keep track of venue, times and the name of the person to contact (and a telephone number). Keep the diary with you in case the venue want to re-book the band and keep the diaries well after they're finished with. Make a note of any special requirements or peculiarities about the gig in case you play them again – so you'll be warned in advance (I know people who keep this kind of information in a computer database). For instance, I played at the re-opening of a club in London years ago which had burned down. The new club had been purpose-designed and so we naturally expected 'all mod cons'. For a start, the club was down an infuriating one-way system and was almost impossible to find if you didn't know the way. Secondly, there was no stage access from the rear of the club, meaning that all the gear had to be loaded through the audience and heaved up onto stage. Thirdly, there was a dressing room on the side of the stage which you could only access from the stage itself, meaning if you were in the dressing room during the support act, you had to stay put. Notes were taken that night, I assure you!

Keep a checklist

Keep a checklist and go through it when you're setting off for a gig. You'd be surprised what it's possible to forget if you're in a rush to get on the road. We once arrived at a gig without the PA power amp...

Enjoy yourself!

And if you can't because of nerves or whatever, practise pretending to enjoy yourself. There's nothing worse than going to watch a band which doesn't look like they're having fun. You begin to wish that you hadn't bothered to come out to see them – and next time you probably won't bother...

Remember that there's a distinction between being a player and a performer. You've practised long and hard at the former, paying a little attention to the latter won't hurt. Audiences have a much better time if it looks like there's a party going on on-stage!

Here's a list of things that I never leave for a gig without...

Torch – stages or the corners of a pub are notoriously badly lit and you do want to be sure everything is plugged in to the right socket! Also, packing and unpacking in dark car parks can be a real case of hit and miss...

Spare strings – a bit of an obvious one, I suppose; but you'd be surprised how many people I've seen caught out.

String changing tools – you'd have thought it was as obvious as carrying spare strings, but I've known people get into trouble in this department. Ideally, you need a string cutter and a string-winder (possibly the best guitar accessory ever invented!).

Spare picks – if you want to look like a real pro, tape a few to the mike stand; picks are very easy to drop and damnably hard to find in the dark. Another good place is on top of your amp – anywhere that's generally in reach.

Tool kit – I made myself up a tool kit which I'd keep with me on gigs. I was accused of being a boy-scout by the rest of the band every so often, but you'd be surprised how often they'd come to me to borrow pliers or screwdrivers! I tried to keep with me all the tools I'd need to deal with minor mishaps as well as guitar allan keys and dedicated tools like that. I was on a gig once where we needed a soldering iron and the bass player said no worries, he'd got one in his car. Now that's class!

Tuner – we've already seen what a godsend these little gizmos are in the practice room, but they're even more handy live. Check your tuning regularly; heat, and the bump and grind of a gig can play havoc with a guitar's tuning.

Spare leads – they're a lot more reliable than they used to be, but it's cheap insurance to keep a spare handy just in case of unforeseen circumstances.

Batteries – if you're using effects pedals, you'll need to carry spare batteries. It's part of Murphy's law that says that a battery never goes when it's convenient for it to do so!

Fuses – there are generally fuse holders mounted to the rear of your amp. Check out their rating (consult the manufacturer if you're not sure) and hunt out some spares from an electrical supplier (a lot of music shops carry them, too). Make sure you've got spare mains fuses, too.

Gloves – we've mentioned this before but it doesn't matter how many times you repeat good advice, in my opinion. Gloves will not only keep your hot, sweaty, just-come-off-stage hands from chilling too quickly and causing medical problems, but will protect them from bumps and knocks. I dropped an amp on my finger once and if it hadn't been for the fact that I was wearing a ring on that finger, I'd probably have broken it. A glove would have helped, too!

more about chords

f you want to further your knowledge of chords, it would still be wise to work to a system so that your development is along a tried and tested route. In the earlier chapter on chords, where we learned how to make the most out of the major, minor and dominant varieties, we covered a lot of ground – it's still a system that will get you out of trouble time and time again, believe me. But there comes a time when a guitarist's knowledge of chords has to be quite extensive. Different chord voicings have a different effect on the music you're playing and a real pro will have a chord for every occasion.

The first thing we can do is to extend our ideas about barre chords. So far, we've looked at two basic shapes:

example 1

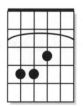 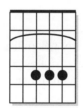

example 2

E maj

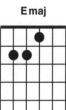

The first looks like the chord of E maj in a root position:

And so this particular barre shape has earned itself the name 'E Shape' – well, we had to call it something. It's far from perfect, as far as a naming system goes, but it's the best we've got, it's pretty universal and so it will do. Having said all that, it won't come as much of a surprise that we call this:

example 3

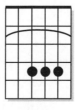

– an 'A shape' barre chord. It is what the chord of A major looks like down at the guitar's nut and that fact alone has given the barre chord its name.

I will add here that names aren't actually that important – well I don't think so, anyway. Just think of these things as reference points, or an easy way of organising information in your head. You need landmarks on the fretboard to help you find your way around, after all.

The barre chord idea actually extends well beyond these two shapes; there are others which are equally as useful as the ones we've looked at, but maybe they don't quite fall under the fingers so easily. Look at this:

example 4

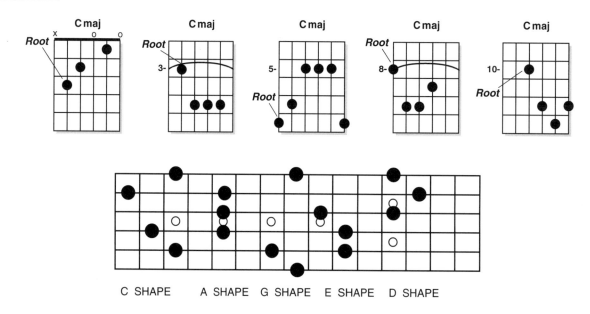

C SHAPE   A SHAPE   G SHAPE   E SHAPE   D SHAPE

Ex 4 is a diagram of where the major shapes fall for the key of C from the first (or 'root') position, right up to the twelfth fret. After that, it just repeats again. You will see some familiar shapes there if you look. Obviously there is the 'C shape' for C, followed by the more familiar 'A shape'. After that, we find the 'G shape', followed by the 'E shape' and 'D shape'.

With sufficient enough stretch, we can turn each of these chord shapes into barre chords. Here's a barre version of the 'C shape':

example 5

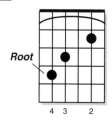

It takes a bit of doing, but it's quite possible with a little bit of effort. Even if you don't end up using the whole shape, it's important to be able to 'conceptualise' sufficiently so that the shapes will be useful to you. Don't worry, everything will start getting clearer in a minute!

The 'G shape' is a real monster to try and play as a barre shape. In fact, it's probably impractical to try and incorporate this shape in anything; but you will find it played 'in bits' all the time. For instance, here's a chord which belongs very much to the 'G shape' barre family.

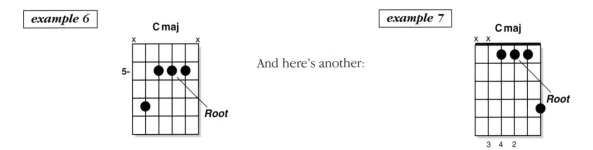

example 6

C maj

5-

Root

And here's another:

example 7

C maj

Root

3 4 2

So you can see that a fully working knowledge of the barre chord system begins to give you an extensive knowledge of chords. Stick with me, it gets better!

After the 'G shape' on the diagram, we find the familiar 'E shape', which we've dealt with previously. Following on from there, we find the 'D shape'. Now this isn't really a barre chord as such and, as far as this system is concerned, the D shape is the runt of the litter.

example 8

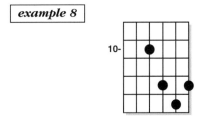

10-

It's still a useful chord shape to know, though.

So what have we got? Five barre chord shapes which go up the fretboard, all extolling the virtues of the chord of C major. But, wait a minute, haven't we got a very usable system here? Think about it again; in the key of C, we first find the C shape, then the A, G, E and D. It spells CAGED – and that fact alone will help you remember it.

Now you remember that the guitar is fabulous as far as moving things around from one key to another is concerned; learn a shape in one place, a scale or chord, and you can repeat the same thing several frets higher and use it in another key. So this particular order of barre chord shapes is applicable to every key? Yes!

Here's the fretboard again, but this time, all the barre chord shapes relate to the key of G.

example 9

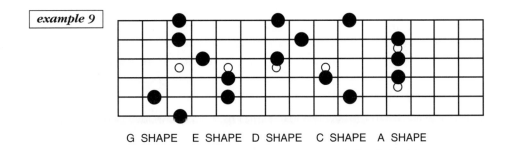

G SHAPE   E SHAPE   D SHAPE   C SHAPE   A SHAPE

Look familiar? Well, if it doesn't at first, you'll be able to see the 'E shape' barre chord for G at the third fret, with the D, C, A and G shapes following closely behind. So the ability to spell the word 'caged' will help you organise this system of barre chords in any key. All you've got to do is remember the order in which the barre shapes progress up the neck and

you should be able to find where you are in any key. You've got the E and A shapes pretty much sewn up by now and so you're really only filling in the gaps.

This system of learning and processing information regarding barre chords has been around since the early 70s and is definitely one of guitar tuition's best-kept secrets!

Making the most of things

Once this system makes some sort of sense to you, you can apply it in all sorts of different areas. For instance, it allows you to learn chords 60 at a time...

Now, nobody believes me when I tell them I can teach them to learn 60 chords at a time without any effort at all, but it's a thing which is well within reach of all of us. Let me demonstrate.

The chord shapes of C, A, G, E and D are all pretty fundamental; you'll certainly find them in every chord book ever written, that's for sure! So when we start to consider other chords, maybe ones that we don't quite know, this system comes in very handy indeed.

Let's take an example. Here's our old friend C major in its root position, down at the guitar's nut.

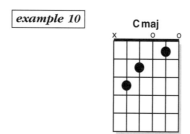

example 10   C maj

You've seen it before, so I'm not going to dwell on it.

Now let's look at how that particular shape is altered to give us the chord of C6...

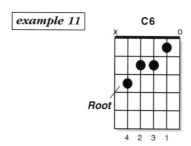

example 11   C6

Root

4 2 3 1

You can still see the familiar C chord sitting there, can't you? We've just added another note to the shape, that's all – we've added the sixth note of C's major scale, that's all. Now, we've just discovered that the C shape barre will move around the fretboard quite happily, turning up at a

different fret location, depending on our choice of key. So that means we can repeat the above chord shape all the way up the neck until we've got a movable '6 chord' shape in all 12 keys. Twelve chords out of one shape? Certainly!

Here's a movable 6 chord shape:

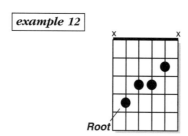

example 12

Root

We've run out of fingers to play all six strings, but the central four strings will be enough to get the idea across very well. Just like with the scales, match up the root notes on your fretboard diagram and you're home free.

But what about the other shapes? Can we use them, too? Here's E6:

example 13   E6

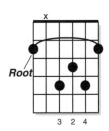

And here's a perfectly acceptable barre chord shape for it:

example 14

Once again, we've got 12 shapes out of one with the full use of the barre system.

When we bring in the other shapes, you can see where the '60 chords at once' principle comes from.

Here's G6:

example 15   G6

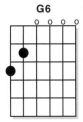

example 16

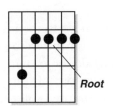

And the barre equivalent:

example 17   A6

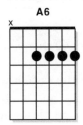

Here's A6:

And here's the moveable version:

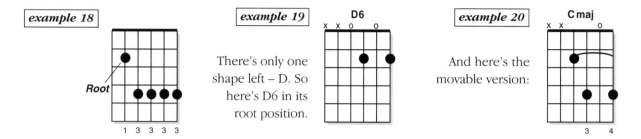

example 18

Root

1 3 3 3 3

example 19

There's only one shape left – D. So here's D6 in its root position.

D6

example 20

And here's the movable version:

C maj

So, we've looked at five chords; C6, A6, G6, E6 and D6 and from them, we've formed movable shapes that will serve us for whatever key we find ourselves in. There are 12 major keys, five shapes – and so my maths tells me that we've got 60 chords altogether!

Of course, it works for every chord. If you wanted a dominant seventh chord for every occasion and key, all you'd have to do is look up the shapes for C, A, G, E and D. Just for the record, here they are...

example 21

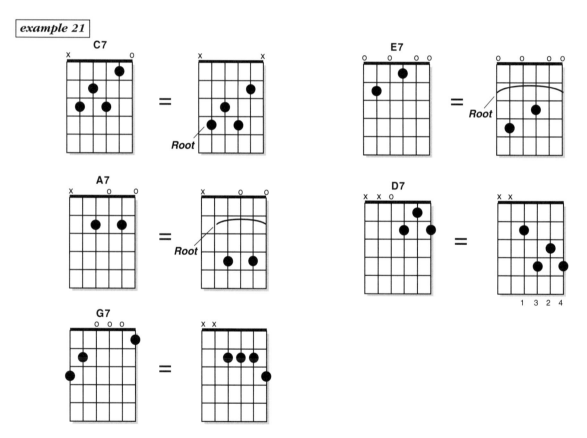

Another 60 chords with little or no effort!

This is the system which most pro players that I know use and it's been around for years. I first discovered this way of organising chords and scales (yes, it works for scales, too!) as long ago as 1981, when I attended a guitar seminar with the great jazz guitarist, Joe Pass. Just being

introduced to the idea of organising chords and scales on the fretboard in this way opened so many doors for me, it became pretty much the foundation of the way I taught from that moment on. I still use it now, in those moments where I'm stuck for a chord voicing on a particular part of the neck and it's got me out of a hole plenty of times!

Quality with quantity?

But why do we need so many chords? Surely just one of each type is enough to get by with? It's true that you can cover an awful lot of ground with just one shape for each chord. But eventually, you're going to start noticing that, despite the fact that the chord you're playing is most certainly the correct one, it still doesn't sound quite like it did on the original recording (I'm presuming you're playing songs you've heard on CD). In those cases, it's the guitarist who has the most versions of the chord in question to hand who wins the big prize. You need a fair degree of intuition in these instances, too; but even that will develop naturally in time.

It's a fairly common question on the part of players new to the instrument and it goes something like it did in part one of this book; how many chords do I need to know? I've already answered the question in the first part of the book,

assuming that we wanted the maximum mileage from the minimum input and we developed a system which would allow us to 'fake it' if we weren't sure of a particular voicing. But, taking this particular system to its logical conclusion, it's possible to answer the question, 'How many chords do you actually know?' with the rather glib, but quite accurate, 'Most of them!'

Treating chords in this way is like having a fairly vast vocabulary; you stumble across words which mean basically the same thing, but only one will probably best convey your thoughts at a particular time. This sort of eloquence – having a pocket full of synonyms available to you at all times – transfers directly to the guitar. Make sure you know several different voicings for any chord and you'll be able to adapt more easily to any given musical situation.

Extending the system

When it comes down to it, every chord in the book relates in some way to the five positions we've looked at, it's just a question of being able to

recognise it at the time. To take one example, look at this chord:

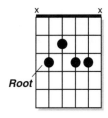

example 22

Your first clue as to its 'parent shape' is the position of the root, which is on the third fret, A string. If you check back, you'll see that two of the 'caged' chord shapes have their roots on that string: the C and A shapes. So, the chord

above must in some way be related to one of them and closer examination reveals that it bears more resemblance to the C shape than the A. It might help if we see the C shape and C9 side by side:

example 23

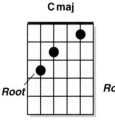 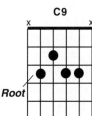

C maj   C9

175

Despite the fact that the two shapes really only share two notes in the same position, they are clearly similar. If we want to be even more on the money, we must remember what we learned about chord families in part one; C9 is a member of the 'seventh chord' family, and so it's going to be a more obvious comparison if we look at the similarities between C9 and C7 at the same position.

example 24

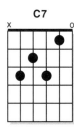

C7

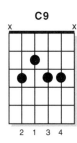

C9

Getting the idea? It's just another way of organising chord shapes in your mind. There are a lot of chords to remember and so some sort of system is going to prove invaluable.

Let's take another example. Here's a C minor seventh chord:

example 25

Cm7

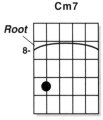

The root note is on the sixth string and only the 'E' and 'G' shapes have their root on that particular string and a little bit of intuition reveals it to belong to the 'E' group. To make it easier, here's C minor and C minor 7 together:

example 26

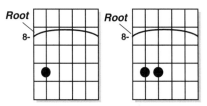

Pretty close family resemblance, wouldn't you say? Apart from being able to structure all this in your head, this way of thinking is another important part of expanding your chord repertoire as outlined above. Now you know that particular minor 7 shape, it's good for 12 keys. But you've still got to know where it fits into the system so that you can always be sure of where you are on the fretboard.

If you look up a chord in a chord book, it's always a good idea to sort out the shape's family heritage straight away because then you can file it away easier in your mind – and will find that you remember it far easier later on.

Chord fragments

It's an easy mistake to make to think that every chord on the guitar has to cover five or six strings. A lot of the time you'll find that you're dealing with fragments of a bigger chord shape. There are loads of reasons why this might be the case; put it down to the 'less is more' principle.

As an example, take a look at this shape:

example 27

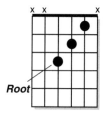

It's an economical, three-note affair which finds its home in the more familiar, much larger E shape:

example 28

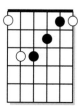

But there are times when the full shape is going to be too much but an excerpt will be right on the money. This is another way that a guitarist can 'edit' himself to provide a more apt accompaniment, rather than charging in with something not quite right.

Taken to extremes, the less is more principle could see you playing an entire blues with two-note chords. Look at these shapes:

example 29

G7
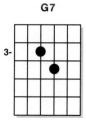

C9
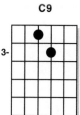

D9
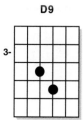

Now look at the bigger versions:

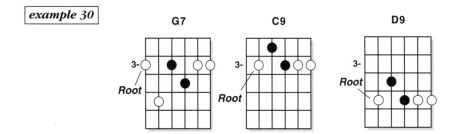

example 30

It's just a coincidence that they all happen to be the same shape and on the same two strings, but it can be an effective accompaniment underneath a laid-back, or restrained blues solo. Try it!

more about scales

There will probably come a time when your thirst for scale knowledge exceeds what we've already looked at so far. It's really a question of vocabulary; the ground we've covered is considerable, in terms of what's in common use in music. But, of course, there's more...

To recap, the vast majority of music that you hear from day to day will be derived from the major scale – that's a fact. So it makes sense to become familiar with the sound of that scale, not only from the point of view of ear training, but also positioning on the guitar fretboard. In the case of the major scale, we've seen that there are five shapes which link together in a chain, or like a big fretboard jigsaw. They also correspond to the five main barre shapes that we looked at in the last chapter. Compare these two charts:

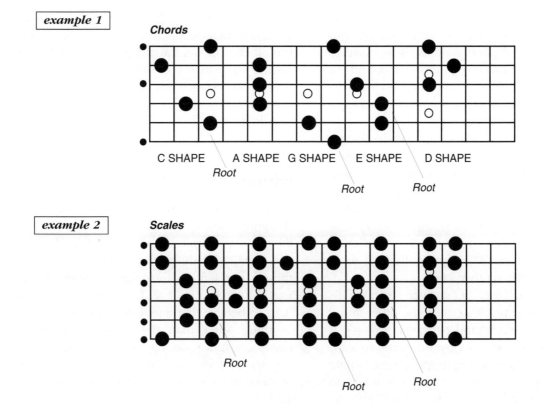

example 1 **Chords**

C SHAPE   A SHAPE   G SHAPE   E SHAPE   D SHAPE

Root   Root   Root

example 2 **Scales**

Root   Root   Root

If you check where all the root notes lie, you'll see that all those chord shapes sit within the scales. Therefore, the next step is to extend your 'filing system' to include the scale shape relative to each chord. That way, you'll be able to find all the major scale shapes going up the fretboard in any key. You're not really learning anything new here, you're really just organising what you've already learned!

As you know, I'm a firm believer in providing 'landmarks' for the eyes and fingers on the fingerboard – and this is probably the most important bit of organising you'll do and so it's worth spending some time becoming fully familiar with it.

After that, turn it round and find all the minor scales (remember, it's basically the same series of shapes looked at from different root notes). See how the majors and minors interlace up the fretboard and remember (once again!) that here is one of the greatest advantages the guitar has over other instruments; we can learn 'shapes' for scales and chords and repeat them in every key. On a lot of other instruments, a new key is a different fingering to remember and so, in general, we have much less work to do in this department.

While we're on the subject of superimposing scale and chord information onto the fretboard, let's spare a thought for the Pentatonic shapes. Here is the major scale, major Pentatonic scale and major chord in a single position:

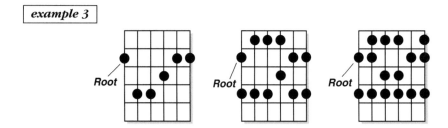

example 3

See the similarity? It shouldn't come as much of a surprise because, after all, we're dealing with the same general pool of notes. If we were to look at this position on the fretboard with all the notes filled in from the chord and both scales, you'd end up with only the major scale, anyway – think about it!

But where to next? Once you're really familiar with the scales we looked at a while back, where's the best place to head for more data? First of all, let's just spend a moment or two thinking what we're going to do by expanding our retinue of scales. We're going to expand what our ears recognise by looking at different contexts of notes. We're going to find some different sounds, in other words.

As we saw in the earlier chapter on scales, it's good to make yourself aware of the other minor scales – the melodic and harmonic variants. It might come as a bit of a surprise to you to learn that I'm not actually going to spend a lot of time talking about these two; I am only going to recommend that you familiarise yourself with the different sounds contained within them. Compare them to the natural minor, see where the differences lie, but tell yourself that it's the natural minor that you will use more often than not. By all means work out some fingerings for them in different fretboard locations, but don't overdo it.

Modes

After looking quite seriously at the straightforward major and minor scales, I usually introduce my pupils to the modes. Now don't go and run and hide at the mention of modes; they're not half as important as some books would have you believe. During the 80s, it was hard to believe that a guitarist needed to know anything other than the modes in order to become a fully-rounded superstar, but it's just not true. Modes are important in their own context, sure – but let's keep an open mind, shall we?

So what exactly are modes? Well, believe it or not, it's just the major scale all over again, just seen from six other points of view.

Let me explain; if we play a C major scale from C to C, we get the familiar major scale sound, right? OK, here's a diagram just for good measure:

example 4

CD Track
42

You've seen it before, and nothing's changed. This scale also has a modal name, the Ionian – so there's one you knew already. But we can also play the same notes from D to D and find a different sound...

example 5

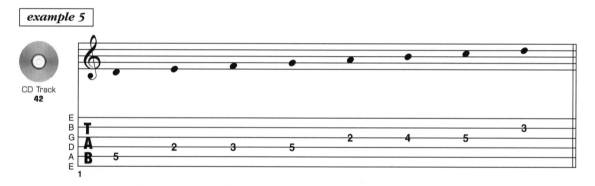

CD Track
42

It's still the same notes that you'd find in C major, it's just that we've altered the perspective a bit by playing it from the second note of the scale, that's all. What we've ended up with is a minor scale which sounds 'sweeter' somehow than the natural minor. It's called the Dorian Minor (you might have heard of it, but don't worry if you haven't). It's strange that, just having 'moved the scale along a bit', we've come up with a lot of different sounds.

Listen to the example on the CD – it's still the C major scale, I promise you!

The most important thing about modes is that you've got nothing more to learn; no new fingerings, nothing. All the modes are contained within the major scale – and we already know that like the backs of our hands, don't we?

So, we've taken C major from D to D and heard the effect it produces, what's next? Try E to E:

example 6

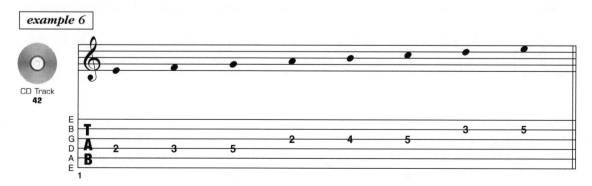

CD Track
42

This one is called the Phrygian Mode and is another minor sounding scale. Without any doubt, the Phrygian's (pronounced Fridge, Ian) major usefulness is when you want to fake some flamenco! On the CD example, I'm playing the E Phrygian over an E minor chord (the chord over which it sounds most at home) and you'd swear I was playing something deeply Spanish, but it's just our old friend C major looked at from a different point of view. Good trick, huh?

Moving along a little, we can play the C scale from F to F (over F major) and come up with a nice twist on the major scale. The sound is called the Lydian Mode and is a favourite of Steve Vai's, in case you're interested...

example 7

CD Track
42

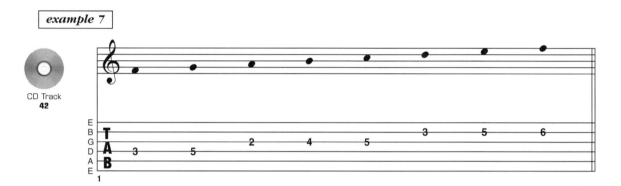

Technically speaking (and I refuse to get too technical about this – so much dross has been written in the name of the modes in the past) we've ended up with a major scale with a twist of lemon; a bitter element in an otherwise sweet-sounding scale. It's a nice scale to improvise with. Steve Vai told me that he'd practically given himself a Lydian hernia on one of his solo albums, so beware!

You might think that I'm being a little off-hand in my view of the modes, but I'm really more interested in you hearing the *sound* they make rather than looking at them from an academic point of view. I mean, you've already learned the major scale and so you know all the fingerings, it's just a matter of re-programming your ear to cope with the slightly different sound the modes produce and you're home free. Think of them coming free with all the hard work you've already done learning the major scale.

Next up, we have the C major scale played from G to G and a heck of a name to remember – the Mixolydian Mode. We've come across this one before, during the workout. But, just for good measure...

example 8

CD Track
42

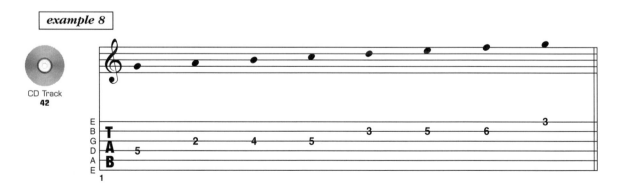

This is another major scale, but it's got a flat seventh, which turns it into the perfect scale for dominant chords. Where the Phrygian was great for pretending you know how to play flamenco, the Mixolydian is wonderful for jazz and funk. It's just that a lot of jazz (and blues, for that matter) features dominant chords and so this scale tends to be something of a jazz staple. Try playing G

Mixolydian over a G7 chord; if you mess around a little with your phrasing, you'll end up sounding like a seasoned jazzer!

If we go one step further and look at C major

from the point of view of A to A, we get the Aeolian Mode, and the chances are that this is going to look very familiar, too...

example 9

CD Track
42

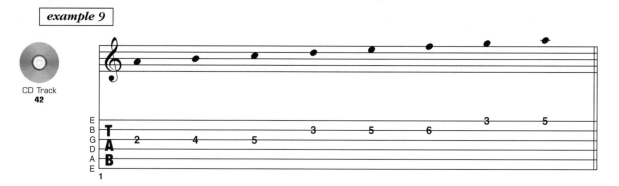

It's the natural minor, isn't it? So you knew three of the modes all along and didn't know it (ie C to C = the Ionian mode, G to G = the Mixolydian and A to A = the Aeolian). This is the kind of thinking I'm eager to promote; knowing all this kind of thing subconsciously without worrying about it, or analysing over much. There is so much dross talked about music, when we start to analyse things...

honestly, I despair!

The final mode is probably the strangest. It's known as the Locrian, but as far as we're concerned, it's just the C major scale played from B to B. The reason why it sounds so oddball has a lot to do with the fact that it's only a semitone away from the real major scale – well, you decide; here it is.

example 10

CD Track
42

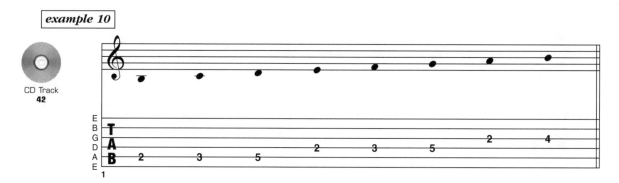

You're probably thinking that you cannot imagine a single case when you'd use such an ugly-sounding scale ever. It's only here from the point of view of completeness. I can't remember ever using it... Except just now on the CD, that is.

So that's the modes, then. Nothing too much to get excited about, I think you'll agree. However much 'extra' you think that you've got from looking at the major scale from a modal point of a view, it's all part of something you already know. The main task is just to tell your ears that. In this sense, it's going to be helpful to you to 'classify' the modes by the way they sound to you, so that you

can call on them from time to time when circumstances demand that you come up with something slightly different. My own classification (if it helps) is this:

Dorian: sweet-sounding minor
Phrygian: portraits of Spain!
Lydian: sour-sounding major
Mixolydian: jazz/funk rules!
Aeolian: the minors strike
Locrian: Er, I expect its mother loves it!

If you want to extend your scalar palette a little, there's no doubt that the modes will provide you with a fair amount of variety with hardly any more work on your part. But I would urge you to concentrate on the Dorian and Lydian modes first; they are the most useful to you (the Aeolian and Mixolydian are very useful, too; but you already know them from the workout). Playing modally calls for a little mental arithmetic from the point of view of playing the right thing over the right chord, but it's really only by experimenting that you're going to find your way. Basically, the Dorian sounds cool over minor seventh chords (of the same name), the Lydian over some major chords (but not all) and the Mixolydian over dominant sevenths in a sort of jazzy, bluesy, funky context.

I don't really want to get any more analytical than that. Improvising with scales is more an 'ear thing' than it is a 'head thing' – although, arguably, improvisation is really a 'heart' thing or 'soul' thing. If you try and play with one eye continuously focused on a guitar tutor, you end up sounding like a human music slide rule.

Anything else?

There are other scales, of course – lots of them. Many have been put together by music academics who feel the need to create a new name for every possible deviation from the norm. You can treat the harmonic and melodic minor scales from a modal point of view, too. You end up with some pretty irregular-sounding scales that way and I would invite you to experiment once or twice, just to see if the sound that's produced in this way is at all appealing to you. The procedure is always the same; take a scale and play it from every note to its octave just to hear what it sounds like.

There are a couple of other scales that are worth mentioning, though, because they do crop up every so often. Bear in mind that we've gone a long way away from what I'd call 'common usage'; these guys are quite refined!

First, there's the diminished scale. This little blighter belongs to the diminished chord, and it sounds like this:

example 11

CD Track
42

Not the prettiest thing you've ever heard, I'm prepared to bet. The fact is, the diminished scale is man-made. It's one of those things that has been academically worked out so that it's symmetrical. In other words, it only contains two intervals, a semitone and a tone, but in the order tone, semitone, tone, semitone, etc. It does come in handy every so often – especially if you want to add a sort of baroque flair to a piece...

example 12
audio only

CD Track
42

The other man-made scale in music is the whole tone scale. It consists of a series of notes which are all the same distance apart and it sounds like this:

Ugly little mother, isn't it? As far as anyone actually using the whole-tone scale in rock guitar improvisation, I can only think of the inimitable Frank Zappa who employed its somewhat dubious charms to any great effect.

Author's message II

Despite the fact that there are many, many more scales to look at and listen to, I've only really got one more to show you. Anything else is going to be a variation of something we've already considered and a good scale book will point you in the right direction if you find yourself drawn towards further exploration. Last, but certainly not least is the scale which contains everything we've looked at in this book, and indeed formed the climax to the workout. If music has an alphabet, it would be this scale that we would recite out loud as we would our ABC. It's the chromatic scale – and I know it will sound very familiar to you...

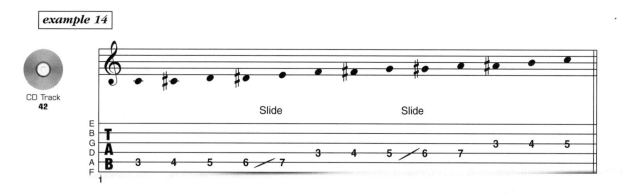

The chromatic scale is everything to music. Twelve notes from which are drawn the most outrageous musical fantasies of every composer who has ever lived. Hence its importance; it is the alphabet for a musician, the very structure over which his every move is made. As an ear exercise it is valuable; being able to sing the chromatic scale means that your ear is attuned to music's DNA and is finally open to all things.

If it sounds like I'm making this scale out to be the Holy Grail, then fair enough; I guess in a way that I am. But what of its significance? If it's so darned important, why have I left it to last in this chapter?

Let's look at it this way; every great novel ever written was constructed from the alphabet, and yet the ability to recite that particular series of letters alone would be irrelevant to a novel's actual construction. The inspiration and power to construct a great literary work goes way beyond such simple matter as the alphabet and the same is true of music. Sure, it's as fundamental and equally important, but at the end of the day it's just another series of notes – and the same is true of any scale. These matters, the naming of scales and all the academic processes which are involved in their definition, come after the event. The creative process lives far beyond the world which seeks to define it. And yet the importance of learning music's ABC cannot be denied. I'd like to think that we're going to keep everything in proportion here and not believe that the ability to play a scale in any key and in any position on the fretboard could ever be mistaken for fine musicianship. It's not; all you've proved is that you can use the machine –

just like you'll remember me comparing typing speed to having anything interesting to say. The two things are completely different.

The reason why I'm making all this fuss about scales, and kind of damning them too, in a way, is because I want people to be able to play music from somewhere deeper than the pages of a text book. I also want to get the point across that, in some ways, music is impossible to reduce to academic formulae. In order to evolve, it cannot be defined; common practices can be observed, but space must always be left for the creative edge to move forward.

Charlie Parker, the great jazz sax player and pioneer was once asked if he had any advice for the would-be musician. His reply is as true today as it was when he said it fifty odd years ago. Learn your scales and theory; then forget all that sh*t and just play!

more about scales and chords

We all know that scales and chords meet up everywhere in music. Call it harmony and melody or whatever, but they're kind of Siamese twins in a lot of ways. Music with either element missing for any length of time stands only a very limited life expectancy.

But what's the *real* connection? If we heave up music's bonnet for a little while and watch her motor running, we stand a pretty good chance of finding out...

We've seen already that chords come from scales anyway. Just to refresh your memory, take any scale:

C D E F G A B C
1 2 3 4 5 6 7 8

Take the first, third and fifth notes from that scale:

C E G
1 3 5

And you end up with a chord. In the case of the above example, we end up with the chord of C major. The scale was C major and those three notes played together best represent the overall tonality which sums up the sense of key which revolves around a scale like moons around a planet. So, if a song is in the key of C major, you're definitely going to run into that chord.

But what happens when a melody is made up only from the notes of the scale? What other chords can we use? If you were to try singing the whole of

the scale over one chord, it wouldn't sound wrong exactly; it wouldn't sound like you were playing any wrong notes, anyway. But it would sound very 'static' and one dimensional. For music to breathe, it demands both melodic and harmonic movement – literally, we have to change chords every so often and the melody has to move, too.

So there are other chords which belong to the scale, apart from just the main, or 'tonic' chord described above and they are formed in pretty much the same way.

We won't get into a big discussion about why those particular notes best sum up a key – it's a debate that could keep us occupied for another book! Just hang on to the idea that all western music is based on harmony which is itself based on chords being constructed the way we've just seen. They've even got a fine word for it: they call it 'tertial harmony', in music's elite circles. (Might be worth dropping into a conversation occasionally, eh?)

So let's find the other chords in our guinea pig key of C major. We've seen that we built the first chord, C major itself, by using a sort of 'every other note' ploy – like this:

C D E F G = C maj

So what happens when we apply this kind of thinking to the other notes in the scale. Take the second note of the C scale, D, and apply the same logic:

D E F G A

And, whaddya know? It's a D minor chord (it's minor rather than major because it contains a minor third – but just take things at face value for a while).

We can take the next note and do the same thing:

E F **G** A **B**

This time, we've ended up with E minor. Now let's take the next few notes and see what we get:

F G **A** B **C** = **F** maj

G A **B** c **D** = **G** maj

A B **C** D **E** = **A** minor

So far, so good. But, as we all know, there's always one isn't there...

B c **D** E **F** = **B** diminished

You remember diminished chords, don't you? Well, there's one up there...

So, if we summarise what we've ended up with just by applying the same rule to the other notes in the scale as we did when we 'invented' C major, this is what everything looks like:

G A B C D E F G

E F G A B C D E

C D E F G A B C

All we've really done is folded the scale back on itself; everything is parallel – at least in terms of letter names. So, having done all that stacking of notes upon notes, what have we ended up with in terms of chord names for the key of C major?

C   major
D   minor
E   minor
F   major
G   major
A   minor
B   diminished

Now, melody and harmony, like two worlds, have collided in one simple experiment. But we've still got a couple of steps to go before we can really see harmony's engine ticking over and the first question has got to be, 'So what do we do with this hat full of chords?'

We discussed a moment ago how a piece of music would sound very dull if the melody was supported by a single, droning chord. Think of a song's structure like a fence; the melody is the horizontal beams, with the chords represented by vertical 'posts'. In actual fact, this analogy is not too far from the truth; chords are vertical if you look at them written on the stave and a melody is horizontal – so there you have it! Obviously a fence supported by one vertical post isn't going to stand up, is it?

We want to escape from the single chord idea and we've certainly enough chords at our disposal to jump the wire, so to speak; it's really just a question of how far to go. If we wanted to, we could support each melody note with a chord, but with melody notes moving quickly through a song, the harmony would seem muddled and much too busy if we changed chord every note – we've got to strike a balance somewhere along the line.

It's time to consult music's handbook for the answer. One of the basic rules of harmony is that a chord doesn't just support one note from the scale, it's capable of supporting more than one. It's a little like our fence idea; the fence posts can be spread out to take the load of the horizontal beams, and the same is true in music. Obviously, you've got to pick and choose your chords – they've got to be pretty sturdy if they are going to support a whole melody...

So we've got seven notes in the scale and seven chords to go along with them – serious option anxiety, huh? Once again, if we consult the music rule-book, we find that a melody note is quite happily supported by a chord which contains it. If we look at three chords from those above, you can see that we've got things pretty much covered in this area already.

C maj = C E G
F maj = F A C
G maj = G B D

If you look at these chords, you'll see that, between them, they contain all the notes of the scale – C D E F G A B – they're all there. So does this mean that just those three chords are capable of supporting a melody in that particular key? Sure does! Isn't science wonderful... But wait, it gets better.

That sort of explains why you might have seen so many chord arrangements which contain just three chords – it used to be called the 'three chord trick' before I was a lad. The trick was that you could write a song as long as you knew these three chords. They occupy the same relative position in any major key, too, and so you can move this sort of thing around as if the whole thing were one huge barre chord.

In order to make this system really universal, and because all major scales are constructed in exactly the same way, we can reduce the whole thing to numbers. The chord built on the first note of every major scale is a major, a minor on the second and third notes and so on. Look at the table below:

Maj	**Min**	**Min**	**Maj**	**Maj**	**Min**	**Diminished**
I	**II**	**III**	**IV**	**V**	**VI**	**VII**

You'll notice that we've used Roman numerals here and that is because music (and guitar, for that matter) is already saturated with numeral-based systems and so we've had to go slightly further afield. Nothing more to it than that.

Now that we've looked at this system (called 'the diatonic system'), we can hear exactly what it sounds like. If you play the chords in a single key up the fretboard, like a harmonised scale, you gain a much better impression of what's happening.

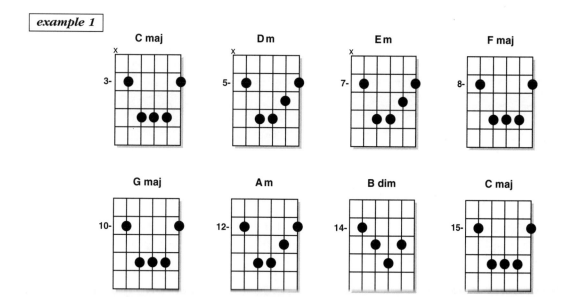

example 1

C maj   D m   E m   F maj

G maj   A m   B dim   C maj

You should be able to hear the scale within the chords.

Of course, chord arrangements aren't limited to three chords. It's quite likely that you'll see the 'VI' and 'II' chords cropping up, too. Out of all of them, the least likely to turn up is probably the 'VII', with the 'III' not featuring too regularly, either.

But whatever happens, all these chords support a single scale – and so the converse is true, too. It means that you can improvise with the C major scale (or major Pentatonic) over a chord arrangement which has been derived from its key.

The principal deviation you'll find is in the area of the V chord. Because of the somewhat mysterious nature of music, the major chord formed on the fifth note of any major scale is commonly converted into a dominant seventh. We've seen in part one how a dominant chord is built on a major triad, the only addition is a flattened seventh. This means that instead of this:

G   B   D   =   Gmajor

You're very likely to come across this:

G   B   D   F   = G7

The F is just another note from the C scale – we've not added any artificial ingredients. It's just that a dominant seventh has a more definitive sound within a chord arrangement than an ordinary major chord. Try it for yourself; first, play this:

| C | F | G | C ||

Then try this:

| C | F | G7 | C ||

The second one sounds like the final C chord is being 'signposted' by the G7. This is, in fact, the main job of a dominant chord; it gives the music a 'homing instinct' and home is the main root, tonic or I chord.

So there you have it; chords and scales have combined together and the foundations have been laid for any musical event you have in mind.

I will repeat, in conclusion, that scales are *not* music in the same way that the alphabet is *not* literature. Both are platforms from which the infinite becomes practically possible.

jargon busters

Every area of life is prone to its own unique system of naming things – or buzz words, if you prefer. So if you want to be able to hold your own in a music shop, or in conversation with a band at a gig, here's a list of some of the more common terms at large in the average guitar player's vocabulary!

On The Guitar...

Acoustic

An 'acoustic guitar' is any non electric instrument which relies upon a hollow body to 'amplify' the sound of the strings. Acoustics usually have steel strings and a truss rod.

Action

The height of the guitar's strings above the fretboard – ie 'I like a high action' would imply that this player likes his strings set quite high above the board. String height is usually adjustable at the guitar's bridge.

Alternate Tuning

Any tuning which isn't the standard EADGBE configuration. Many acoustic players use other tunings in their compositions, and many electric guitarists drop their bass E string to D for super-grungy chords!

Archtop

Typically, a jazz guitar where the top of the body is 'arched' or contoured in shape.

Bolt On

The method of attaching a guitar's neck to its body via bolts – as opposed to a 'set' or 'glued in' neck.

Bottleneck

A glass or metal tube worn over a player's finger in order to play slide or bottleneck guitar. So named because early bottlenecks were, in fact, the necks of bottles!

Bottom String

The geography of the guitar is nothing if not contrary! The bottom string is the bass E – it's actually the one nearest to you as you sit with the instrument in the playing position. So called because it's the lowest in pitch – hence 'bottom'.

Bridge

The metal or wood assembly which marks the end of the strings' playing length at the body end of the instrument. The bridge can adjust intonation and string height.

Capo

Short for Capo D'astra, a little sprung device which a player attaches to the guitar neck to hold down all the strings at a certain fret. For example, if you attach a capo at the fifth fret of the guitar, you would have a set of 'open strings' consisting of ADGCEA. Useful device for changing a song's key without all the unnecessary maths!

Down The Neck

In the direction of the nut. Seeing as the regular position of the guitar has the neck pretty much horizontal, this directive can cause an awful lot of confusion!

Electro-Acoustic

This usually implies an acoustic guitar which has been fitted with an internal pickup in order to amplify it. It can also mean an electric guitar with a hollow body. Although the two definitions could be seen as being the same thing, there is a subtle distinction; the first has the appearance of an acoustic guitar with hidden electronic assets, the second is outwardly a regular electric guitar which benefits from some acoustic characteristics, too.

Electronic Tuner

Possibly the best invention for the guitar in recent years! Plug your guitar into one of these clever little devices and it'll tell you if you're in tune or not. They are digital, too, and more accurate than the human ear can ever hope to be. Buy one.

F-Hole

Literally 'f' shaped holes either side of the strings on instruments like violins and cellos. Jazz guitars have them, too. Alternatively-shaped soundholes.

Fine Tuner

An idea pinched from the violin world. A set of tuners at the bridge end of the guitar with a limited range (the main job is still carried out at the headstock end) to keep the guitar tuneful when you have a locking trem on board.

Fixed Neck

Another way of saying 'glued in'. An alternative to bolting the neck to the guitar body (see 'Bolt On').

Floyd Rose

Floyd Rose is actually a person! But his name is now used as a generic term for a locking tremolo system. Rose was first on the block with the necessary patents for the idea, you see.

Fret

The metal bits on the fretboard. It's the frets which 'stop' the string and produce a pitch – fret positioning and stability is critical.

Fretboard

The wooden playing surface of the guitar's neck. Fretboards are usually either maple, rosewood or ebony, but there are quite a few alternatives.

Fretboard Radius

The degree by which the fretboard curves from one side to another – a bit like the camber or convexity of a road surface.

Headstock

The part of the guitar which carries the tuners – and the manufacturer's name, of course!

Heel

The bit at the back of the guitar where the neck and body join. On classical instruments, this can be quite an ornate affair, but the humble electric boasts many different shapes and sizes.

Intonation

A full explanation is, as they say, beyond the scope of this book, but generally speaking, a guitar not only has to be in tune with the rest of the band, it has to be in tune with itself. The intonation is adjusted at the guitar's bridge and is brought about by altering the strings' individual length. Don't meddle, leave adjustment to someone who knows what they're doing or until you're sure of your ground.

Jack Plug

The metal connector at each end of a guitar lead which connects an electric guitar to an amplifier.

Jack Socket

The socket on both a guitar and an amplifier where you insert the jack plug.

Locking Trem

See Floyd Rose. In the wild days of tremolo usage, players complained that guitars kept going out of tune, mainly due to friction at the nut. Floyd discovered if you actually lock the strings down at the nut, put some fine tuners on the bridge, things remain a lot more healthy.

Neck

The playing area of the guitar which comprises fretboard and frets.

Nut

One end of the strings' vibrating length, down at the headstock end of the instrument. Nuts used to be made from bone or ivory, but now synthetics rule the day!

Nylon String

A colloquial term for a classical guitar, which has nylon strings instead of metal.

Pick

See 'plectrum'.

Pick-up

An electromagnetic device (traditionally a combination of copper wire and magnets) which turns string vibration into minute voltages which are fed in turn to an amplifier and made much too loud (usually).

Plectrum

A piece of shaped plastic used to strike the strings.

Position Markers

A lot of guitars have markers at the third, fifth, seventh, ninth, 12th, 15th, 17th, 19th and 21st frets. They are there more for the sake of simple orienteering rather than anything musically profound!

Pots

Colloquial term for the guitar's volume and tone controls. Derived from the word 'potentiometer'... you can see why they shortened it.

Retro-Fit

Term applied to any modification made by a guitar user after purchasing an instrument ie, 'It had a vintage trem on it when I bought it, but I retro-fitted a Floyd Rose.'

Scale Length

The distance between a guitar's nut and bridge ie the vibrating length of its strings.

Scratchplate

Plastic plate fitted to the front of a guitar to protect it from bumps, knocks and, well, scratches when in use.

Semi-Acoustic

Usually an electric guitar which has a hollow body (see 'Electro Acoustic').

Slide

Another word for 'bottleneck'. Can also be applied to playing the guitar with the left hand holding a metal bar to stop the strings.

Solid Body

A guitar body made from either a single piece or a composite of several pieces of wood to form a solid mass. Most traditional electric guitars have a 'solid body'.

String Gauge

The diameter of a guitar string, usually measured in thousandths of an inch (despite desperate attempts to have the guitar world go metric. No chance, matey!). A top E string is quite likely to be .009 gauge, whilst its bass counterpart with probably weigh in around .042. You'll hear guitarists ask for 'A set of 9 to 42s' in shops. Don't worry, it's still safe to talk to them.

String Saddle

The part of a guitar's bridge where the string crosses it.

String Tree

A little device on a guitar's headstock which holds the string in place and makes sure it crosses the nut at a good angle (ie, it won't rattle or do anything else which might be considered unsociable).

Toggle Switch

A device on an electric guitar for switching between pickups or combinations of pickup.

Top String

More confusing guitar geography. The string which is highest in pitch, ie top E string. As you hold the guitar, the top string is the one nearest the floor. I didn't make the rules...

Tremolo

The mechanical device for altering the pitch of a note or chord. Tremolos are nearly all based on spring tension vs string tension and pivots and stuff. 'Tremolo' is not the correct term anyway, as 'Vibrato' means slight altering of pitch and tremolo means slight alterations in volume. It's daft, but it's never been corrected!

Tremolo Arm

The lever on a trem bridge which the player controls the pitch adjustment; press it in towards the body and it lowers the pitch of all the strings, pull it away from the body, it raises the pitch.

Truss Rod

A steel rod down the centre of an electric or steel-strung guitar to strengthen it against the rigours of string tension. It's adjustable, but there's one rule: don't. OK? Let someone who knows what they are doing adjust it for you only if it's really necessary. You'll be glad I told you that one day.

Twelve-String

A guitar with 12 strings! Actually, it's six *pairs* of strings which are tuned in such a way that the effects of playing one of these guitars can be quite mesmerising. They tear your fingers to pieces, incidentally...

Up The Neck

Towards the body, pickups and so on. So called because you're going up in pitch.

Whammy Bar

A colloquial term for the tremolo arm.

Pick-Ups...

Active

Pickups which require on-board circuitry and a battery to produce a signal for the amplifier. Usually thought of as being more 'hi-fi' than conventional 'passive' pickups.

Coil-Tap

A means whereby one of the coils of a humbucker is effectively switched off to give the player a single coil sound.

Humbucker

A pickup which has two coils (as opposed to a single coil's one) and two sets of magnets. The idea is that one coil's magnets are set north to south, the other's south to north and that not only gives you higher output (ie more volume), but it cancels out annoying hum at the same time.

PAF

Stands for 'Patent Applied For'. When the Gibson guitar company started using humbucking pickups on their guitars, they applied for a patent, hence pickups from this period in Gibson's history are known as PAFs. Guitar voodoo dictates that they sounded better than any humbucking pickup since. Plenty of attempts at recreating the PAF's classic tone have met with varying degrees of success.

Passive

Not active. Needing no on-board power source ie the ordinary, bog-standard magnet and wire device.

Polepiece

The magnetic metal lug which sits directly under a guitar string producing an magnetic field in which the string vibrates and produces a minute current for the amplifier to turn into Armageddon...

Single Coil

The opposite to a humbucker. One coil of wire, one set of magnetics, no noise-cancelling facility, but it's a classic noise. Probably.

Stacked Humbucker

A single coil and humbucker hybrid. Literally, two coils, but on top of each other. Hence, all the benefits of a humbucker with the physical dimensions of a single coil. Useful for retro-fitting single coil guitars.

Staggered Polepieces

Vintage Fender pickups had their polepieces set at different heights in order that their output be constant from string to string. Thought to define a sound epoch in electric guitar.

Vintage

Usually, any guitars or associated paraphernalia from the 50s, 60s and now (unbelievably) the 70s is regarded as being vintage. Used as a synonym for 'good' a bit too often. (Get a real, vintage sound, etc.)

Wrap

The material used to surround the magnets in a pickup ie copper wrap. Archivists go silly about the amount and consistency of wrap on vintage pickups. No comment.

Amplifier...

Boost

An electronic means to vary the amount of distortion present in an amplifier's output.

Bottom End

The bass end of the frequency spectrum.

Cabinet

The housing for the speakers which are attached to the output of an amplifier.

Combo

A single unit combination (hence 'combo') of amplifier and speakers.

Decibel (dB)

A ratio between noise and electrical current, courtesy of Alexander Graham Bell. Apparently. More commonly used to measure speaker output – beware it's a logarithmic scale which means that 96dB is quite loud, but 120dB will induce pain. So watch yourself.

DI

Stands for 'Direct Injection' where a guitar is fed directly to a mixing desk in a studio, bypassing the use of an amp.

Effects Loop

A special output and input at the back of an amplifier to which you can connect your effects units for better performance. Far too complicated to go into the electrical reasons why here!

EQ

Equalisation... basically the treble, middle and bass controls (and any other refinements, for that matter) on your amplifier.

Feedback

Another deeply complicated electro-acoustic phenomenon which has been turned into an art form by certain guitarists! Basically, it's that electronic howl you get when you're standing too close to a powerful (ie loud) amp. You can do tricks with it.

Four By Twelve (4x12)

A colloquial term for a cabinet containing four twelve inch (diameter) speakers. Also known as a 'fourbie'.

Gain

Another word for 'boost'.

Head

An amplifier which is designed to sit atop a speaker cabinet ie, it doesn't have its own speakers.

High End

In EQ terms, it means treble and above.

Hot Rod

An amp which has been modified in some way, usually to produce even more volume. Gawd.

Master Volume

Once upon a time you had to turn an amp up really loud before it would start to distort (ie sound good), but in the 70s a way was found to produce distortion without the accompanying high volume. So they gave you one volume to determine the amount of distortion and a Master Volume to control the amp's overall output.

Midrange

The frequency band which sits squarely between treble and bass – middle, y'see?

Power Amp

The part of an amplifier which is dedicated to producing ear-battering volume. Ouch.

Pre-amp

The part of an amplifier which is dedicated to forming the tone contours (and a few other niceties) of a guitar signal before being passed onto the power amp section.

Reverb

Traditionally, a set of springs which delay the signal slightly within an amplifier to produce the sort of ambient effect to be had by playing in a cathedral without the inconvenience of actually playing in a cathedral...

Speaker

An electro magnetic device – the final step in the guitar/amp interface – which actually produces all those notes we're trying to get right.

SPL

Stands for Sound Pressure Level and is a way of measuring how loud something is by looking at how much air it's moving. Roughly.

Stand By Switch

Used on valve amplifiers to shut down part of the circuitry when the amp is not needed, but you don't want to switch it off (in a break, for instance, between sets). It has the effect of protecting the valves and preserving their life.

Transistor

An amplifier with no valves in it! A furious debate raged once (probably before you were born) about which was better, transistor or valve amps. Valves won.

Twin Channel

An amplifier with two independently adjustable channels so you can theoretically set up two completely different guitar sounds – one for rhythm and one for lead, perhaps.

Valve

An electromechanical device, better known to its friends as a thermionic valve which can be used in electronic devices to achieve different feats and acts of derring do. They sound great, OK?

Vintage

Anything amp-shaped with valves in it! (See 'valve' above.)

Watts

Another system of electronic measurement which, loosely, defines an amp's power output. Once again, like decibel, it's logarithmic and so 100watts is only twice the output of 10 watts. Crazy.

Effects...

Analogue

Good, old fashioned, pre-digital age, no nonsense thingummies full of recognisable electronic components. Not that I'm at all biased, you understand. Vinyl LPs were analogue audio.

Digital

Take a signal, convert it into numbers, maths and stuff, and you can do anything you want to it. In theory. CDs are digital audio.

Distortion Pedal

Generic term for any device which produces or imitates the sound of an amp at full whack without the inconvenience of ensuing deafness.

Effects Chain

The order in which you string together several different stomp boxes.

Fuzz-Box

Older, more 60s, terminology for a distortion pedal. They didn't work quite as well, but it didn't seem to bother Hendrix.

MIDI

Mnemonic for Musical Instrument Digital Interface, a language which different digital effects units use to talk to each other. Clever.

Multi-Effects

A single unit which contains a lot of different effects.

Patch

Hangover terminology from the pioneering days of music synthesis where different devices were 'patched' together via electronic matrices. Trust me, I was there. Now, it means a combination of effects active together to produce a desired sound.

Pedalboard

Guitarists who used several stomp boxes at once soon found themselves experimenting with DIY and nailing (in some cases) stomp boxes down on a piece of board to make them easier to move. Things have become more sophisticated since (in some cases).

PSU

Power Supply Unit. Dedicated, mains power supply for your stomp box collection. Saves you bundles of money buying batteries, otherwise.

Rack

The alternative to floor mounted units, 'rack' effects are stack mountable in custom units (some the size of domestic refrigerators and beyond).

Stomp Box

Colloquial term for an effects footpedal – you have to stomp on them to turn them on or off, y'see.

Volume Pedal

A footpedal which controls the volume of your instrument. Handy, if you're too busy picking to play with the guitar's on-board volume control.

Wah Wah

A footpedal which was originally designed so that a guitar could make the sound of a muted trumpet. It's a tone filter which produces a sound like a 'wah' when rocked back and forth.

Techniques...

Alternate Picking

The basic form of picking which guitarists use to play melody lines, solos, etc. Basically, it means that if you start with a downstroke, you follow it with an upstroke and so on. There are exceptions to the alternate picking rule, though, so stay sharp!

Bending

The art of pushing or pulling a guitar string across the guitar neck to raise its pitch. An indispensable technique for playing practically any style of guitar.

Damping

See muting.

Dive-Bomb

An extreme downwards pitch swoop using a whammy bar. If you're really skilled with a tremolo, you'll even get the sound of a small explosion at the end of a dive when all the guitar strings go slack and hit the pickup with a bang!

Double-Stop

Essentially, playing two strings at once.

Downstroke

A downwards playing movement with the plectrum.

Hammer-on

A technique whereby after the note is played, a finger from your fretting hand 'hammers' onto the fretboard to produce a note higher in pitch (see What Special Techniques Do I Have To Know?) without re-picking.

Harmonic

Technically, a node point along the guitar string which, if touched lightly with the fingertip and gently picked, will produce a note harmonically related to the note usually found at that fret.

Muting

Limiting the resonance of the guitar strings using the flesh of either the left or right hands.

Pull-off

The opposite to a hammer-on. A note is played in the normal manner, but then the fretting hand finger is 'pulled off' the string, which has the effect of sounding a note below it without re-picking.

Slides

Picking a note and sliding the finger either up or down the guitar neck without re-picking.

Slur

Playing two or more notes with a single pick stroke either by hammering or pulling.

Tapping

Using the picking hand to fret a note by tapping the string on to the fretboard.

Upstroke

An upwards picking motion with the plectrum.

Vibrato

Slight (or sometimes not so slight) variation in pitch of a note brought about by side-to-side movement with the fretting finger.

Music...

Arpeggio

Literally, the notes of a chord played one after the other rather than all together.

Barre Chord

A chord which requires all the strings to be stopped using the first finger.

Blues Scale

A hybrid scale which contains all the notes found in a blues. Exact definition is open to controversy!

Chart

Colloquial term for a chord arrangement written out for band members ie 'chord chart'.

Diad

Two notes played simultaneously – not quite 'big enough' to be called a chord. Shame.

Dominant Seventh

The flattened seventh note of scale. Also, a chord built on the fifth note of a scale.

Fifth Chord

A diad that thinks it's a chord! Usually the interval of a root and fifth played as accompaniment to many a rock'n'roll anthem. Because the 'chord' doesn't contain a third, it can be defined as being either major or minor, depending on context.

Flat Fifth

The flattened fifth note of a scale. Important note in the blues. In medieval times they thought playing it invoked the devil – silly buggers...

Key

The determining factor which assigns a piece of music a tonal centre, or a sense of belonging to a particular scale.

Major

A scale or chord which contains a natural third (ie the chord C major contains the notes C, E and G).

Minor

A scale or chord which contains a flattened third (ie the chord C minor contains the notes C, E♭ and G).

Part Barre

A chord where several (but not all) of the strings are stopped using a single finger on the fretting hand.

Pentatonic

A scale which contains five notes.

Scale

A pre-defined series of notes which ascend upwards and downwards in steps ('scale' actually means ladder. Neat, huh?).

Seventh Chord

A chord which has the formula root, third, fifth and flat seventh – also known as a 'dominant seventh'.

Stave

The series of five parallel lines onto which music is written.

Tablature

The series of six parallel lines which represent the strings of the guitar onto which fret positions are indicated in guitar music.

Time Signature

The 'fraction' at the beginning of a piece of written music which indicates its rhythmic nature. The most common is called 4/4 which implies four beats to the bar.

Miscellaneous

Ball-End

The brass ring at the end of a guitar string which stops it slipping through the hole you've just threaded it through!

Cord

Americanese for a guitar lead. It's catching on over here fast. Resist people, resist!

Drum Machine

Around the end of the 70s research began to find a machine which could replace a drummer... Nowadays 'virtual drummers' are heard everywhere, the most sophisticated containing samples of real drums recorded in pro studios and programmed to reproduce precision drum patterns. They still haven't invented one that drinks Guinness, though!

Flight Case

Essentially, a specially reinforced instrument case thought to be able to resist the caring caresses of airport baggage handlers world-wide!

Gig

A concert or performance put on by a rock'n'roll band. The term has expanded, however, to include many different areas of employment.

Lead

The cable which guitarists use to connect their instrument to an amplifier.

Mixing Desk

The console which forms the central matrix of a recording studio or PA set-up. You feed all the instruments into the mixer, adjust the volume level, eq and many other refining niceties before unleashing all on an unsuspecting, weary public.

PA

Short for 'public address' which is an amplification system (quite usually of awesome power) which all the instruments and vocals in a band are fed through for concert performance.

Wireless System

A radio link between instrument and amplifier (a sort of 'virtual lead') which only really comes into its own on huge stadium stages where a trip-over-your-lead type of pratfall could fatally indent one's pride!